MAN OF HONOR

HOW TO BE A HERO
TO THE WOMAN IN YOUR LIFE

JIM COTÉ

InterVarsity Press
Downers Grove, Illinois

InterVarsity Press
P.O. Box 1400, Downers Grove, IL 60515-1426
World Wide Web: www.ivpress.com
E-mail: mail@ivpress.com

©2004 by Jim Coté

All rights reserved. No part of this book may be reproduced in any form without written permission from InterVarsity Press.

InterVarsity Press® is the book-publishing division of InterVarsity Christian Fellowship/USA®, a student movement active on campus at hundreds of universities, colleges and schools of nursing in the United States of America, and a member movement of the International Fellowship of Evangelical Students. For information about local and regional activities, write Public Relations Dept., InterVarsity Christian Fellowship/USA, 6400 Schroeder Rd., P.O. Box 7895, Madison, WI 53707-7895, or visit the IVCF website at <www.intervarsity.org>.

All Scripture quotations, unless otherwise indicated, are taken from the New American Standard Bible. Used by permission. All rights reserved.

Design: Cindy Kiple

Images: medal—Steve Cole/Getty Images
couple—Scott T. Baxter/Getty Images

ISBN 0-8308-3210-6

Printed in the United States of America ∞

Library of Congress Cataloging-in-Publication Data

Coté, Jim, 1953-
Man of honor: how to be a hero to the woman in your life/Jim Coté
  p. cm.
Includes bibliographical references.
ISBN 0-8308-3210-6 (alk. paper)
1. Bible. O.T. Ruth—Criticism, interpretation, etc. 2. Boaz (Biblical figure) 3. Ruth (Biblical figure) 4. Men—Biblical teaching. 5. Man-woman relationships—Biblical teaching. I. Title.
BS1315.6.M2C68 2004
248.8'42—dc22
                                                              2003027938

| P | 17 | 16 | 15 | 14 | 13 | 12 | 11 | 10 | 9 | 8 | 7 | 6 | 5 | 4 | 3 | 2 | 1 |
| Y | 16 | 15 | 14 | 13 | 12 | 11 | 10 | 09 | 08 | 07 | 06 | 05 | 04 | | | | |

To whoever wants to be a hero, especially his wife's hero.

To every man who aspires to be God's champion to his family, first to his wife, then to his children as he has the privilege of being a father, and finally to his "clan" and greater community, from which he comes and to whom God has called him to serve.

To every principled man who has discovered that there is no higher honor than serving those you love and those who are dependent on you.

To those who believe there is no greater joy than seeing your family healthy and secure within your leadership.

To the men who know that there is no higher calling in family life, in the Christian life, than being your family's hero, that is, God's man of honor.

CONTENTS

Introduction 9

1 Healthy Men, Family Heroes 15

2 Real Men, Bull Riders or Not 24

3 A Real Man Is a Provider—*Ruth 1* 35

4 A Real Man Is a Pastor—*Ruth 2* 53

5 A Real Man Is a Protector—*Ruth 3* 68

6 A Real Man Is a Patriarch—*Ruth 4* 87

Afterword 106

Notes 117

INTRODUCTION

You've probably never heard of Kris Kime. He was just a normal guy, not a celebrity or anybody famous. But to six families in the city of Seattle, Kris is a hero.

What started as a day of fun at Seattle's version of Mardi Gras turned into a frantic fight for life. Twenty-year-old Kris Kime spotted a woman who was being attacked by a group of young bullies. He tried to intervene, putting his own life in jeopardy as he sought to rescue the defenseless woman.

The attackers turned on him. Though the woman escaped, Kris became the focus of the assailants' irrational anger. They hit him on the head with a bottle and beat him repeatedly. The blunt force caused Kris to lapse into unconsciousness.

The ghastly affair was caught on videotape and later replayed on the local news. Two people who watched the beating and then hoped for Kris's survival and recovery were Rick Allison and Larry Levinson. What these two men had in common is that they were themselves fighting for life; both were awaiting organ transplants. Rick needed a lung transplant because his lungs were ravaged by pulmonary fibrosis. Larry was suffering heart failure and only days away from death. Elsewhere in the Seattle area, attorney Martha French needed a pancreas, and Jesse Bettes and Ray Page were both awaiting kidneys.

Unfortunately, Kris didn't make it through the ordeal. His injuries were fatal. However, Kris was thoughtful enough to have made himself an organ donor. So out of the failed attempt to save one woman, his sacrificial death provided life for five terminally ill people.

Later, some measure of justice was served in that Jerrell Thomas, an eighteen-year-old thug and one of the assailants, received a prison sentence for his role in Kris's death. Though Kris's family was present at the trial, real solace for them came when they spent time with the people who had received his donated organs.

Kristen, Kris's sister, later said that she saw a little of her brother in all five of the organ recipients. Jesse Bettes called the whole affair a miracle. But perhaps Rick Allison summed it up best when he called his new set of donated lungs "hero lungs." One man died attempting to save a life and in his death provided life for so many others. Rick Allison is right—Kris Kime is a hero by anybody's standards.[1]

Heroes don't have to be famous celebrities. Heroes are simply people who do the heroic thing whether it's a deed big or small. By an average citizen's standards, they do what is extraordinary. And in selflessly risking danger to serve a person in need, they ultimately excel where most people shrink back. That's why they get our attention and admiration.

I want to dwell on that concept a moment. Consider the idea of a hero. Heroes selflessly risk their own personal safety or comfort. They put themselves into difficult or dangerous circumstances simply because someone is helpless and without help will suffer unnecessarily. Heroes, then, are those who put personal resources to bear in a less-fortunate person's life, often at great cost to themselves. They are by nature sacrificial and become by effort redemptive—buying back the precious life of the one whom they intervened to rescue.

Heroes can be military greats, political figures or business tycoons. But they can also be average, everyday garden-variety people like you and me who might put themselves in harm's way to help others. More often than not, heroes are ordinary people doing extraordinary deeds because they serve a cause bigger than themselves.

This book is about the concept that a man needs to be a hero to the woman in his life. We don't have to be rich, famous or bigger than life to do that. We just need to be willing. And we need to get into the fray if we are going to prove our heroism and by so doing express our manhood fully.

Many men in America today are giving family life their best shot. Men are working hard, bringing home their pay and forgoing personal pleasure in order to take care of their families, leaving precious little for their own personal development or recreation. To be sure, there are some real screw-ups in our society, as evidenced by the pornography business, the divorce rate, increasing prison populations, the abuse of women and children, child abandonment, child support delinquency and so on. Many men have lost their view of heroism as it relates to the family. These males are grossly underperforming their masculine responsibilities.

Perhaps that is what's wrong with the moral state of American society. Many men have dropped the compass of a biblical direction for pursuing masculinity. As a result, men are wandering lost in a thicket of behavioral options that forest our social landscape. Today's popular network sitcoms typically portray men as relational, intellectual and financial ignoramuses who are focused predominantly on sexual interests and little else. Couple that with the modernist propaganda assault against traditional male roles, and we find that many men have lost all concept of what it means to be an exemplary male. After all, what does "male" mean?

Despite the cultural acceptance of "male bashing," God has an elevated role for men. And this book is dedicated to the notion that we can actually fulfill it. You see, rather than ridicule there is a reverential role for men, a God-given and a God-honoring one. But it is one that you will be hard pressed to hear today if you listen to popular media and their humorous but denigrating portrayal of us.

That's why I find Kris Kime's story so compelling. That young man not only demonstrated community heroism; he gave us a videotaped view of a real man. He exercised true masculinity. And it cost him a lot—in this case his life. True heroism and real manhood are always costly because virtue never comes cheap.

So what is the solution? How can we learn to be heroes in our own right?

We need to know our identity. We need a solidly biblical definition of our gender as well as the parameters of our role. We also need a concrete, practical example, a role model who helps point the way to excellence and gives us someone to emulate.

So to you men who are hacking through a thicket of misinformation about gender roles, to those of you who are dedicated to your wives, families and communities, I applaud you. I am cheering for you to maintain your persistence as you gain a clearer view of what it means to fulfill your God-given design.

However, though persistence is a virtue, persistence is not enough. Unlinked to truth and divorced from an appropriate target we are apt to persist to our exhaustion. Then we will later discover that we have not accomplished the best, the highest, the noblest of achievements. A compass is only as good as the one who reads it and adjusts his path properly to the direction it provides. In order to hack successfully through the thickets of gender confusion we need a clearer sense of what God expects from a man if we are to reach our destination victoriously.

So to persistence I want to add revelation. We men need to know the truth about how God views our role and responsibilities if we are to develop a clear understanding of who to be and what to do with our lives.

I wouldn't want any of us to persist in a direction that isn't on compass. Even a few degrees off of dead reckoning can move a man inextricably into a quagmire of missed opportunity, failed effort and regret. If we want our lives to count fully as God evaluates a life, we will need his direction. Fortunately he has provided us with just the information we need to get us and keep us on target. God's design for men is unmistakable. Though each man's process and progress will differ according to his unique challenges, nonetheless each man's target is the same—to fulfill his design according to the perimeters and role God has given.

So let's go there, to the perimeters and to the role model. And when all is said and done let's take the next step to achieve biblical masculinity and male nobility, that is, to be men of honor. Let's become heroes to our wives and those within our sphere of community.

CHAPTER 1

HEALTHY MEN, FAMILY HEROES

What kind of a family did you grow up in? Was it healthy, stable and honorable? What kind of father did you have? And did he honor your mother?

Those are tough questions to ask and answer because every family has a huge set of complexities that make it unique. Those uniquenesses make pat answers to complex issues seem very trite. It is not easy to compare the health and stability of one family with another because there is no standard in our society to compare to. Therefore generalizations are dangerous and solid conclusions often evasive.

Your father may have divorced your mother. But the way he handled it during and after the fact may seem to you to have been fairly honorable.

On the other hand, your father may still be married to your mother, yet she may be enduring one of the most difficult men on the planet.

Your father may have spent little time with you because of the demands of his profession. Yet the time he did spend may have affected you so thoroughly for good that your memories of your upbringing with him are warm and wonderful.

Or your dad may have been with you a great deal—yet his anger, irascibility, domineering attitude and impossible-to-please perfectionism may have left you wishing he would hike off to another planet.

Every story is different. Often a father's influence in the family's life, for good or for ill, is "in the eye of the beholder." Since every man has both positive and negative attributes, finding a suitable contemporary role model for masculinity as it relates to marriage and family isn't easy.

I once met a widow whose husband, facing an impregnable wall of debt after years of financial reversals, decided to kill himself. Yet the way he prepared the family emotionally and financially convinced them that it was an honorable act, even redemptive. They see his death as a "loving sacrifice" by which he "in the giving of his life" enabled his loved ones, his wife and children, to overcome their financial problems and secure a better future.

So this is the dilemma in trying to find an honorable or dishonorable male role model for the principles of noble masculinity. Every family has its skeletons because every family is filled with humans. Families are congregations of people who sin and sin regularly. In fact, most of us are very adept at sinning. Personal failures can mount, building a heritage of family dysfunction.

So where do you go for health and balance?

My own upbringing had enough ups and downs that I hesitate to use my experience. We were an average family by most standards in the '60s and early '70s. I don't think there is anything extraordinary to report there. On the other hand my wife, Brenda, grew up with incredible parents and enjoyed an especially wonderful role model as a father. He was certainly a hero to her and her sister as well as her mother. But she would blush if I used her story, so I won't. Instead let me illustrate some of the positive characteristics that I believe are part of a healthy and responsible family leader. That way I won't needlessly embarrass those closest to me.

WINSTON CHURCHILL:
Breaking the Cycle of Dysfunction

It may surprise you, but one good example is Winston Churchill. I have always admired him as a husband of honor because of the almost complete about face that he accomplished as a married man. Winston did not grow up in a particularly healthy or happy home. His parents, though cordial, were often separated. His mother, Lady Randolph or Mrs. "Jennie" Churchill, was a known lady of profligacy. And during their estrangements she was well known to occupy the attention of many men.[1] And her husband, Lord Randolph Churchill, known in political circles for his opportunistic penchant rather than a commitment to "coherent corpus of beliefs,"[2] did little to correct the situation—because of his work load, his poor health, her independence, his neglect or perhaps all of the above.

Young Churchill, then, was essentially raised by his nurse, Mrs. Everest, whom he regarded more a real mother than his actual mother. Also, his family's finances were a continual strain. His father, a politician and Member of Parliament, had a reputation for a huge ego and big mouth but mediocre political ability and so alienated himself from many of his peers.[3] This cast a negative shadow on Winston when he at last entered his life's work as a Member of Parliament himself. So the whole of his relationship to his parents can be summed up best in the words of one of Winston's biographers, Roy Jenkins:

> Winston Churchill's non-relationship with his father was even more wistful than was his semi-relationship with his mother. Lord Randolph was too exhilarated by politics during his period of success and too depressed by them (and by

his health) during his decline to have much time for parenthood. . . . The most poignant comment on Winston Churchill's relations with his father is that which he is reported to have made to his own son, . . . in the late 1930's when that Randolph was twenty-six or seven. They had a long and maybe fairly alcoholic dinner together, alone at Chartwell. Towards the end Churchill said: "We have this evening had a longer period of continuous conversations together than the total which I ever had with my father in the whole course of his life."[4]

But how was Winston's home life once he married? His marriage seemed to be one of genuine love. There is a rather romantic story told about him as a result of a comment he made during a banquet of attending dignitaries. They were all asked to answer a hypothetical question:

> If you could not be who you are, who would you like to be? Naturally everyone was curious as to what Churchill, who was seated next to his beloved Clemmie, would say. After all Churchill could not be expected to say Julius Caesar or Napoleon. When it finally came [sic] Churchill turn, the old man, the last respondent to the question rose and gave his answer. "If I could not be who I am, I would most like to be"—and here he paused to take his wife's hand—"Lady Churchill's second husband."[5]

This fairly well sums up his public reputation as a husband. It reinforces the fact that he was not only a hero to countless Brits for his stand against Hitler and Nazi Germany during the Second World War but that he was also a hero to his wife.

JOHN ADAMS:
Exceptional Modeling Despite a Demanding Career

John Adams seems to have been truly a family man in every sense of the word, even though he had one of the most strenuous, costly and lengthy political careers in our nation's history. Through much of it he endured lengthy separations from his wife and children, living in Europe and soliciting governments favorable to the American cause of freedom as we sought our independence from England.

John and his wife, Abigail, enjoyed one of the best though most public marriages in American history. This short quotation from her recounts:

> My dearest friend [which she affectionately called him throughout their 45-year marriage]: How much is comprised in that short sentence? How fondly can I call you mine, bound by every tie which consecrates the inviolable friendship yet separated by a cruel destiny, I feel the pangs of absence sometimes too sensibly for my own repose.
>
> There are times when the heart is peculiarly awake to tender impressions, when philosophy slumbers, or is over-powered by sentiments more conformable to nature, It is then that I feel myself alone in the wide world, without any one to tenderly care for me, or lend me an assisting hand through the difficulties that surrounded me. Yet my cooler reason disapproves the ripening thought, and bids me bless the hand from which my comforts flow.[6]

John Adams didn't write as much or as poetically about their relationship as Abigail, but a short passage from his diary gives us a sense of his feelings toward her. He would speak of her as his Diana, the

Roman goddess, addressing her in the privacy of correspondence as "Ever Dear Diana." The following short extract from his diary gives us a glimpse of his feeling for her while courting.

> Di was a constant feast, tender, feeling, sensible, friendly. A friend. Not an imprudent, not an indelicate, not a disagreeable word of action. Prudent, soft, sensible, obliging, active.[7]

Then decades later, his love for her steeled into a personal moral code, he would counsel his own daughter about the kind of character to look for when courting a man.

> Daughter! Get you an honest man for a husband, and keep him honest. No matter whether he is rich, provided he be independent. Regard the honor and moral character of the man more than all other circumstances. Think of no other greatness but that of the soul, no other riches but those of the heart. An honest, sensible, humane man, above all the littleness of vanity and extravagances of imagination, laboring to do good rather than to be rich, to be useful rather than make a show, living in modest simplicity clearly within his means and free from debts and obligations is really the most respectable man in society, makes himself and all about him most happy.[8]

John Adams embodied not only these sentiments but these virtues. During his separation from Abigail in Europe, a period lasting over four years, he remained faithful to her and the family. Others of equal public renown, namely Thomas Jefferson and Benjamin Franklin, were not known to exercise the same degree of fidelity. So in the end Adams, like Churchill, was both a national as well as family hero, especially to his wife.

TEDDY ROOSEVELT:
Fierce Leader but Compassionate Family Man

And we could go on to recount the family life of Theodore Roosevelt, whose devotion to his children is legendary.[9] His faithfulness to his wife is embedded in history, proving that wealth and prominence are not a guarantee for domestic failure. A man can achieve a full and significant career without sacrificing his family duties, and "Theodore Rex" proves this fact with distinction. But he remains another historical figure. Isn't there anybody closer to our generation?

Sure there are. You probably know a few.

HOWARD HENDRICKS:
Walking the Talk

I count Howard and Jeanne Hendricks as my friends. I got to know the Hendrickses through their son Bill, who is a close friend and a coauthor of my first book. But I've grown to admire Howard and Jeanne over the years.

They are both world-renowned speakers who maintain an incredible speaking and traveling schedule. Howard travels over 200,000 miles a year. In addition, he holds a distinguished professorship at Dallas Theological Seminary, the chairmanship of the Center for Christian Leadership and board positions for numerous Christian ministries. In other words, he is a busy professional. But he hasn't let that dethrone him from the higher position of being a family man and husband.

My admiration of the Hendrickses began when Brenda and I first moved to Dallas in 1981. We began to read their books *(Heaven Help the Home* and others) and listen to Howard on a radio program called The Art of Family Living. Years later, after establishing a ministry to married couples who experience a lot of business travel, I had the privilege of interviewing the Hendrickses for a videotaped product entitled "Marriage and the Road." Their candid responses to the difficult questions young couples asked about marriage elevated my esteem for their wisdom. Their off-camera interaction behind the scenes cemented my respect for them. Howard is a personal hero of mine and a treasured mentor to countless others who have been blessed by his ministry at Dallas Theological Seminary.

But most important, he is his family's hero. Listen to the words of Bill Hendricks, who knows his father best, warts and all.

> My Dad is well known for his emphasis on family life. For years, he has taught a course at the seminary—now legendary—called Christian Home. Likewise, he has authored several books on the topic. The irony is that he did not really have a model to follow for how one builds a solid family, let alone one established on Christian principles.
>
> So in a way, our family was a sort of laboratory for him. I mean that he actively and intentionally tried to live out the truths that he was discovering in Scripture for how one "manages his household well," to use Paul's phrase. I can remember family devotions at the breakfast table. Bible studies and discussions during our vacations. Faithful attendance at church and Sunday school. Prayers before meals, trips, major undertakings, and at milestone events. Bible memorization. Challenges to uphold Christ-like values. Observations on the issues of the day. Admonishments to treat our Mother with respect and our siblings with kindness (that was an especially hard one to get across!). Exercises in goal-setting. Modeling the value of hard work. Projects for sharing the gospel. Programs for handling our allowance money. And many

other activities, too numerous to mention.

My point is that my Dad did more than just talk a good game—he got in the game! He didn't allow the lack of a model or a meager amount of instruction to stand in the way of doing his best. First he studied his Bible, then he prayed, then he acted. For sure, not every "experiment" was successful. A few never took off, and one or two even blew up on the launch pad. But if, as they say, the only real failure a man can have is to never have tried, then my Dad was a very successful father indeed![10]

So can a man be a hero to his wife and family? Not only *can* he, he *ought* to be! A man is called, designed and equipped to be a family and community hero—a man of honor. And now we have some popular and contemporary models that show it can be done.

Now we are ready for a little revelation to reinforce this issue from the perspective of authoritative, divine truth. Let's begin our discussion of what it means to be a man of honor by looking at our ability to perform this elevated state of manhood. Let's look first at the design issue. Then we'll search the Scriptures for concrete principles upon which to build our own family legacy of honor and nobility.

CHAPTER 2

REAL MEN, BULL RIDERS OR NOT

What does a man who operates out of his creation and calling by God look like? Let me paint a picture by way of illustration, and then we'll apply it to ourselves.

THE BULL

Wow, what a magnificent sight. As I rounded a curve on a country road in North Texas, I slowed the car down to a crawl in order to take in the scene a little more closely. There he was, a Texas-sized Hereford bull in all of his glory. In the meadow was a small herd of cows, and upon a knoll twenty or thirty yards from them stood their leader.

He looked confident and competent. He was huge and he was in charge.

He seemed to be watching the hillside surroundings as if he was guarding the cows. His eyes showed his intensity though his body, statue still, wasn't moving. He certainly wasn't daydreaming—he was alert and intimidating.

His stature was regal. He looked to be in complete command of his responsibilities as if he dared anyone to interrupt his dominion. The exquisite, oxford-brown creature had a huge head supported by a short massive neck that flowed into and stopped abruptly at the front of a muscular body that looked the size of a small bulldozer. The chunky front legs, which seemed capable of trampling a compact car, were joined to a robust torso that flowed smoothly into hindquarters and legs that dwarfed the fence posts holding the strands of wire that separated him from me. Out alone on that mound of rock and dirt next to that narrow strip of highway there was nothing in the vicinity that was a match for his imposing physical strength and fixed attention. I wasn't about to challenge him, and I don't think my car would have won in a head-to-head battle either.

What a trophy of God's creation. He was an incredible specimen of muscular tissue and bold confidence. Here was an impressive bull, behaving as his creator had intended, naturally acting out his design and completely content (from my vantage point anyway) with the situation and, no doubt, the rewards. As my car slid slowly past his sentry's position, I realized that here in Texas some men actually ride those things. In fact, my own son has! I am sure that it is an adrenaline rush like no other and has probably earned him some additional "admiration capital" amongst his friends, especially the ladies. But the jury is still out, in my mind, as to how smart it is.

I have a feeling that bull riding isn't really about admiration capital. It challenges our sense of strength, endurance and athleticism. Maybe conquering a bull for eight seconds helps us to put some perimeters on our physical strength, which for many men is the measure of their masculinity.

Oh, I know it is not so for all men, but most men have some sort of performance standards—financial, athletic, sexual or professional—as a measurement of their masculinity. But is that the best way? Is it even right? Where can we get a sense of the fulfillment of our male design if not by manly contests of achievement?

This competitive, conquering spirit unfortunately leads men to social isolation rather than peer acceptance.[1] Through the years, at least in this country, it has become the behavioral norm for defining masculinity, especially for the insecure male who believes his identity and significance are wrapped up in his achievements. The resulting social phenomenon is that men mistrust one another as they size up each other for class dominance. Because the threat of failure or the fear of defeat keeps men at arm's length from each other, we define the highest form of masculinity as a man who can go it alone and pick himself up by his own bootstraps—a kind of dominant, independent, isolated, but semi-civilized gorilla. This self-sufficient "animal" characteristic is the new paragon of maleness. He was a "bull" in his own right, alone, on top of the hill. The strongest male, "the big man," means the guy on top, who needs no one but himself. That is the popular portrayal of the superior man.[2]

In fact, in America in the past two centuries, this stereotypical male image became a historical pattern for our heroes. We valued the Lone Ranger who didn't need to rely on anyone. He could go it alone and achieve personal success. Historically it seemed our founding fathers embodied this when they launched themselves into the untamed wilderness of this continent to establish our nation. And the media has reinforced this concept with its portrayals of heroic men. Some of the silver screen's most prominent role models were Jeremiah Johnson (Robert Redford), Texas's favorite son, John Wayne, and others like Clint Eastwood, Sylvester Stallone and of course the inimitable James Bond, 007.

I caught some of that contagion myself. When I grew up becoming a man had to do with initiation into certain exploits. Coming of age meant killing your first buck, getting a driver's license and then building a fast car. For some it meant drinking their first six-pack and then stomaching harder stuff. For many in the '70s becoming a man meant having your first sexual experience—and that expectation hasn't changed much in the decades since. But that isn't the sum total of masculine actualizing as one moves from boyhood to adulthood, is it? Then what is it?

That answer will take some time and thought, because the achievement of masculinity as revealed in Scripture proves to be a process whereby males learn to exert their unique gifts in society in an honorable and not self-serving fashion. And that is the thesis of this book.

But we need to begin at the beginning. I want to make a couple of fundamental observations about males in general. These assertions are about our created design, physical makeup and physiology, and they help define our role in society.

The first assertion is that *God created us male* (Genesis 1:27), distinct from our female counterpart. That is not an insignificant observation, though it seems so obvious. Much has been made of gender differences to date, so I will leave you to read other authors whose works offer far more depth than we have room for here.[3] But I do want to say this; men are hardwired for ruggedness and adventure. And the internal drive that keeps our motor running is fueled by the hormone called testosterone. Testosterone helps give men the impetus they need to be builders, warriors, hunters and other aggressive enterprisers that require high energy.[4]

Second, *God created us to act* (Genesis 1:28). We are created and commissioned to initiate constructive achievement, to pierce the frontiers of our formidable environment and pioneer improvements in our world as direct stewards of our creator. Our orders are essentially to civilize by cultivating our fallen world, exercising our stewardship dominion with dignity, responsibility, reverence and gratitude before the God who owns it all and supervises every life.

This "he" hormone, as James Dobson calls it, is a biological fact inherent in our design and corresponds functionally toward the accomplishment of our stewardship. I believe it gives us a hint of God's intent for males. We have more than *permission* to take on the challenge of our formidable world; we are *commissioned* to use our natural energy in constructive ways that benefit our families and greater society. Dobson says,

> Men on the other hand [over against the female temperament and nature] have been designed for a different role. They value change, opportunity, risk, speculation. And adventure. They are designed to provide for their families physically and to protect them from harm and danger. . . . This is a divine assignment.[5]

So does riding bulls make us men? Of course not. But it is just like a man to want to ride one. It can be an outlet for exercising our temperament and design. Left at that there is certainly nothing wrong, in my opinion, for getting hitched onto one of those exploding freight trains and having the ride of your life. I just don't think I would do it. Surfing, yes; bull riding, no.

Anyway, I find that many men, especially young men, are not only struggling with a working definition of manhood. They can't seem to find a clear illustration by which they can view their gender role in a positive light—especially if their dads have failed them somewhere along the way. Consider, for example, my buddy Matt's comments during a recent counseling session at Starbucks.

A Typical Story

Matt (not his true name) is a single 39-year-old, filled with sincere spiritual zeal and a fighter pilot's mentality for adventure. He was resonating with excitement as he quoted from memory the thesis of a popular men's book. He was all exercised about the notion that he had permission to pursue honor and significance through adventure. For the first time he felt liberated by a Christian author to be a "real man" and use his energy without apology.

Then he shocked me with his honest, insightful and transparent comment about his disgust with many of his Christian buddies. He said something to the effect of, "Man, where can I find some real men to hang out with, some guys who are willing to pursue a little adventure? All of my married buddies drive minivans, stay in their neighborhoods on the weekends and won't play golf because their wives would never allow it. What's happened to them? Where can I find some male friendships that exude confident masculinity and a zeal for Christ and his church? These guys are *emasculated!*" Honestly, those were his words, not mine!

I couldn't believe it. I just about dropped my cup of coffee. Little did Matt know that I was that day in the process of addressing that very subject in this chapter. Matt speaks for many men I come across both in and out of the church who feel the same way. They want to connect with other men. I suspect they want to discover masculinity afresh in today's politically correct society without losing their unique identity as men created to perform a God-ordained role.

What does that mean today? How do you act male today with any sense that you're living by an accurate definition, since the gender debate has left the subject of "definition" completely up for grabs?[6] And how does marriage influence the role and responsibility of a man who now has greater domestic responsibilities than when he was single?

Perhaps it is time to overturn the socially accepted ambiguity and the dysfunctional definition of a Lone Ranger male that many men currently operate by. We need a biblical model of a healthy male identity for our world to observe.

Matt, at least, was the first guy who put the issue in such forceful and unpretentious terms. It also coincided with a study I was currently engaged in Scripture. Coincidence?

So we talked and I tried to settle him down.

"Matt," I said, "your desire for fulfilling male relationships in the context of legitimate masculinity and biblical Christianity is admirable. Your feelings about the feminization of men in the church, I believe, is accurate or at least is felt and documented by other well-meaning and highly educated but frustrated Christian men today.[7] But the solution is not to castigate your buddies for cultural adaptation. Goodness, I drive my wife's minivan from time to time, for heaven's sake! Don't adopt a secular view of masculinity from the chest-beating machismos of society. After all these married friends of yours are exercising their stewardship in ways you do not yet understand.

"It would be wise," I continued, "first to understand what God delineates as the fundamental responsibilities of a man as well as his unique God-designed role. Then and only then can we properly evaluate behavior and choices to see if these are masculine or not, by God's standards, not ours. Then and only then will we be able, with confidence, to develop a lifestyle and adopt friendships that will be fulfilling. Then we'll be men of honor."

TIME OUT: What Is Honor, Anyway?

Before we go any further a brief explanation of the word *honor* is in order. Our English word is derived from the Latin for *honor*, *honos; official dignity, repute, esteem,* eventuating in the English meanings: "**1.** high regard or great respect given, received or enjoyed; esp. glory, fame, renown, good reputation, credit **2.** or a keen sense of right and wrong, adherence to action or principles considered right, integrity 3. a reputation for chastity 4. high rank or position."[8]

These are the characteristics that men should be displaying in everyday life. Many men are doing this already. Unfortunately, many men do not realize that this is the male legacy that we've been endowed with by our creator. These are the attributes that should envelop our definition of masculinity. These principles cause men to be heroes to their wives and families and provide noble leadership to the community at large.

So when we discuss the concept of men being heroes and that we ought to be our women's heroes, please don't mistake the origin of this high calling. Though many a woman delights to know that her man is a hero of biblical proportions—which we shall spell out in the chapters that follow—I am not saying that men should be heroes because women need a hero per se. I want to say that the attributes of a hero are the hallmark of a real man because God has called us to this lofty position. We were created to perform at this level. It is a divine mandate, not just a sociological benefit.

God has endowed men with sufficient latent gifts and drives to enable us to achieve this calling. But they must be discovered and developed. Men don't become heroes accidentally; they become heroes on purpose. And in the process we not only honor God with our obedience as we comply with his plan, but we also win the hearts and minds of our wives and children as we serve them as men with honor.

We are to pursue true manhood because God called us to. It is theologically binding. It is not only a utilitarian obligation to be masculine because it is beneficial to our wives and greater community, though it ultimately does just that.

BACK TO MATT AND THE BIBLE

How did Matt and I wind up our conversation? Well, it went something like this.

"Matt," I said, "adventure, assertiveness, aggressiveness and other dominant traits of the stereotypical male need to be harnessed within the virtuous constraints of God's stewardship for men. We can't define masculinity by today's social standards because our sense of right and wrong will change with each generation's new behavioral emphasis. We also need to be careful of any definition that resonates only with our flesh, what Paul refers to in 1 Corinthians 2:12-16 as the natural or 'psyche' man. Males operating out of mere biological or cultural impulses, without a biblical basis for behavior, will behave carnally. They—we—will do whatever feels good, what's legal and what's acceptable by society's standards, but that isn't pure enough for God. He expects more of men."

"So where," Matt then asked, "do men find a balanced perspective on masculinity? I mean, I want to do what God wants, but I don't believe that God wants me to be a wuss. I have both physical energy and a heart that wants to know and please God. I want to engage challenges and succeed and not just succumb to cultural expectations. So where do we go for balance?"

"Great question," I responded. "Men need to operate from a spiritual, or *pneuma*, condition—a submission born of a spiritual relationship with the living God, our creator and redeemer. With sin in our world and in our lives, we can't afford to operate only on a natural level; we must be governed by the Spirit. That is the first step to a balanced model of masculinity. Then, second, we need to use our God-given strength and aspiration for success within the confines of a God-given mandate for responsible living. And the specifics of that are found in the pages of Scripture.

"Think about it," I finally suggested. "Who says that lifting a four-wheeler is manlier than driving a minivan or a Honda Accord? Who says rappelling off monstrous rock formations is manlier than playing with your kids in a sea of plastic balls at McDonald's?

"If we are to find a fulfilling expression of masculinity we have to evaluate that standard from a fixed point of reference."

"All right, I get it," Matt admitted. "Just because some of the things I was taught in the past were too tame, biblically speaking, doesn't mean I am justified in now defining manliness by the popularity of chest-beating macho models of this generation—does it?"

"No it doesn't, my friend, but I can relate to the tension of trying to find the balance. Here is what I've learned . . ."

WHERE'S THE TRUTH?

Men, if you can identify with the tension of finding a balanced view of masculinity, and if you agree that it's confusing trying to find a successful, working definition of appropriate male behavior in a society that has too few role models and too many bogus answers, then follow me through this next comment: You and I need to build our perspective on masculinity from a trustworthy source of information. And to find that, we have to go to the inerrant Word of God.

Let me hasten to admit that my thoughts are not the end-all on this subject. But I have found four fundamental areas in which males are responsible, before God, to perform. They give us an appropriate view of masculinity and help us frame a proper balance of what it means from God's perspective to be a responsible male.

These four responsibilities are the determiners, biblically, for evaluating manhood. Each male has a life, a sphere of influence, a divine commission that he must contend with as a leader and initiator. And these four fundamentals are the hallmarks by which his measure of success will be evaluated. They do not represent the sum total of a man's many opportunities to obey God and succeed in society, but they do represent a man's four primary responsibilities. And should a man abdicate his role here, he will miss his calling and force untold hardship on those he is connected to in life.

Fortunately, in looking for an overview of a biblical job description, we don't need to read through the entire Bible; we can find a complete overview in the pages of one short, four-chapter book, a narrative of two men and two women. The two men are set in apposition—one an object of failure because he tried to operate on the outskirts of his role, the other an inspiring success because he operated within what God had called him to do.

And the women of this story? They were the victims and the beneficiaries of the men's performance. When they were engaged with the first man, their lives were a miserable wreck, filled with loss, disappointment, grief and shame. But when they were connected to the second one, the real man, they were blessed beyond description by his faithfulness. And amazingly, the beneficial results have been passed down to you and me today—literally, as we will see.

But I am getting ahead of myself. Let me simply introduce you to an excellent model for masculinity, a man who through his faithfulness to this fourfold responsibility is a man worth imitating today.

So, readers, without further delay, let's begin his story in the next chapter.

CHAPTER 3
A REAL MAN IS A PROVIDER

Ruth 1

Heroes, models, men to copy. In the contemporary world we look at stars for inspiration and guidance—athletic stars, movie stars, Wall Street financial stars, political stars and the like. The problem is, as I read the front page of today's newspaper I notice one universal characteristic—they are all falling stars!

For example, consider the crisis of confidence in American business as one large company after another and one executive after another is being sued for erroneously stating the company's financial statements. Some of the largest corporations in America mismanaged shareholders' equity by attempting to manipulate the stock market through fraudulent accounting. By off-booking debt and miscategorizing expenditures, thus inflating earnings and profits, and then selling their stocks before their real earnings truth came out, these corporate pirates hoped to rake in millions of dollars for their personal profit. The list of executive liars and their companies reads like a who's who of Wall Street darlings: Enron, WorldCom, even brokerage house Merrill Lynch and Big Five accounting firm Arthur Andersen are just a few who are under investigation for fraud. No doubt some of their big boys will go to jail. But a couple of years ago they were the heroes of investment portfolios, the keynote speakers at posh banquets and celebrated in money magazines. Now what are they? Losers! And so are those who collaborated with them.

But it seems like there is always some crisis of confidence in our national celebrities or institutions. A few short years ago it was our infamous president Bill Clinton. Now it's business magnate Jack Welch or home design maven Martha Stewart. Tomorrow it will be somebody else. Someone is always disappointing us with their human foibles or indiscretions. Even our biblical heroes have moral warts and character limitations. They all make us pause before we consider using a modern or ancient figure as a model to emulate.

STARS TO FOLLOW?

For example, Bible students might point to King David as a model leader and mighty warrior who balanced well on the tightrope of private worship and public service. But he made big mistakes and suffered the shame and ignobility of adulterer, murderer and absentee father. So his example is a little hard to digest.

Abraham is another hero to the religious community. But alas, for all his successes he was guilty of abdicating major leadership decisions in his responsibility to his wife and personal calling before God. Perhaps his hesitation to stand up for his responsibilities helps explain why he lied about his marriage, saying that his wife was his sister, as he offered her as an addition to a political competitor's harem. It was a chump's way to save his own skin.

The prophet Daniel? He was a man of impeccable character and business acumen. But he never married, so it's hard to relate.

And the blue-collar fishermen of the Gospels? They were so erratic, even as apostles, that one must pick and choose carefully for replicable techniques they displayed in their attempt to live successfully, as we must do for all of those mentioned above.

So who can we look up to as an example of masculine responsibility? There are probably several, but one in particular gets my attention. Of all places, he is found in the historical period of the judges, when social chaos and moral relativism reigned in Israel.

What's funny about this character is that at first reading he is easy to overlook. I found him as he lay hidden behind the main plot and characters of a book written about two women. The book, titled with a woman's name, discloses the plight and rescue of these two women, their inheritance and ultimately the lineage to the Savior. But the person who acts as God's instrument to faithfully carry these women to safety is a nondescript, middle-aged farmer by the name of Boaz. He doesn't make a single mistake in the narrative, so I believe that makes him a good character study for us. He provides a practical, realistic example for negotiating life's challenges successfully. Boaz is just a normal guy. He is not an unearthly power. He is no mythological Greek god. He is simply a good farmer and a good example.

You know, farmers often get a bad rap. They are immortalized by the familiar "farmer's tan" you get when you're outside all day with a T-shirt on and only your neck and arms are exposed. Not too many years ago a bestselling book portrayed the love-starved, sensual yearnings of a farmer's wife as she fell headlong into a lurid affair, justifying it all because her faithful husband, steady and dependable as he was, wasn't as cosmopolitan and romantic as his philandering competitor, a traveling photojournalist. But though the farmer ended up the victim, he was in my estimation the real man of the story, unglamorous though he may have been.

So it is with our main character Boaz. He doesn't seem to have the flash and panache that thrills women and inspires imitation in men as, say, Elvis did. But he did have an asset that is in meager supply with most celebrity males today. Boaz was consistently faithful to his full range of responsibilities and could be counted on to do the right thing, the best thing, for others while fulfilling his commitments, even at great cost to himself. He was redemptive as well as responsible. We will see him using his financial resources to purchase freedom for two women without the necessary means to help themselves. He makes for a great character study, I believe, when one is trying to find a practical example of what true masculinity might look like.

ATTEMPTING A DEFINITION

Masculinity isn't really defined by culture or demonstrated by muscle. Nor is it gained through the number of women sexually conquered or by athleticism, military, financial or political victories. The kind of masculinity I've been looking for is a clear representation of real manhood fleshed out in the course of everyday life. So let's try to frame a definition. What is a man? How do you define simply the basic performance expectations of our gender?

Let me take a stab at a definition of masculinity as I condense the components of true manhood down to their most basic ingredients. Ready? I believe a real man is defined simply as *a male who lives responsibly*. I know, it's not too imaginative, but think about it.

Since it takes no talent at all to be born male and since we don't even have a choice in our gender biology, then the difference between males must be how we behave, not how we are constructed. Since so many males act badly and since the Bible promotes goodness as both an admirable characteristic as well as a moral reflection of our creator, performance standards must be the hallmark that separates the men from the boys.

A Real Man Is a Provider

If boys play with trucks and men work on them and drive them, then in the sphere of virtue we can expect a similar demarcation. Mere males live selfishly but men live responsibly. Men work at doing things God's way. Men put others first and themselves second as they serve the whole of their sphere of influence under the ultimate authority of God. That's being a man of honor. It's the first step to being your woman's hero!

Virtue is what separates men from mere males. And this behavior must be purposeful. It will encompass God-revealed standards for behavior as set forth in Scripture. And it presupposes that we will operate fully within the stewardship arena that he has provided each of us individually.

Therefore I have chosen the short definition above because it encompasses both divine standards and human obligations. It is stated simply because I believe the Bible presents the summary of our stewardship that simply. We are to live (1) *as God designed us* (in our gender identity), (2) *as God informed us* (through his written revelation) and (3) *as God endowed us* (in his gift to us of a specific stewardship arena). We do this knowing God will eventually evaluate us.

In short, man is most masculine when he moves toward responsibility in the four stewardship arenas that God has entrusted to him. And of all biblical books, the book of Ruth most clearly and succinctly shows us not only what those four fundamental stewardships are but illustrates how to pursue them successfully in ordinary life by using an ordinary man as the model. This historical record of Boaz's life will help show us what it means to be a real man.

So let's begin by reading the first chapter as the curtain opens on a sad state of affairs.

Ruth 1

¹ Now it came about in the days when the judges governed, that there was a famine in the land. And a certain man of Bethlehem in Judah went to sojourn in the land of Moab with his wife and his two sons.
² The name of the man was Elimelech, and the name of his wife, Naomi; and the names of his two sons were Mahlon and Chilion, Ephrathites of Bethlehem in Judah. Now they entered the land of Moab and remained there.
³ Then Elimelech, Naomi's husband, died; and she was left with her two sons.
⁴ They took for themselves Moabite women as wives; the name of the one was Orpah and the name of the other Ruth. And they lived there about ten years.
⁵ Then both Mahlon and Chilion also died, and the woman was bereft of her two children and her husband.
⁶ Then she arose with her daughters-in-law that she might return from the land of Moab, for she had heard in the land of Moab that the LORD had visited His people in giving them food.
⁷ So she departed from the place where she was, and her two daughters-in-law with her; and they went on the way to return to the land of Judah.
⁸ And Naomi said to her two daughters-in-law, "Go, return each of you to her mother's house. May the LORD deal kindly with you as you have dealt with the dead and with me.
⁹ "May the LORD grant that you may find rest, each in the house of her husband." Then she kissed them, and they lifted up their voices and wept.

¹⁰ And they said to her, "No, but we will surely return with you to your people."

¹¹ But Naomi said, "Return, my daughters. Why should you go with me? Have I yet sons in my womb, that they may be your husbands?

¹² "Return, my daughters! Go, for I am too old to have a husband. If I said I have hope, if I should even have a husband tonight and also bear sons,

¹³ would you therefore wait until they were grown? Would you therefore refrain from marrying? No, my daughters; for it is harder for me than for you, for the hand of the LORD has gone forth against me."

¹⁴ And they lifted up their voices and wept again; and Orpah kissed her mother-in-law, but Ruth clung to her.

¹⁵ Then she said, "Behold, your sister-in-law has gone back to her people and her gods; return after your sister-in-law."

¹⁶ But Ruth said, "Do not urge me to leave you or turn back from following you; for where you go, I will go, and where you lodge, I will lodge. Your people shall be my people, and your God, my God.

¹⁷ "Where you die, I will die, and there I will be buried. Thus may the LORD do to me, and worse, if anything but death parts you and me."

¹⁸ When she saw that she was determined to go with her, she said no more to her.

¹⁹ So they both went until they came to Bethlehem. And when they had come to Bethlehem, all the city was stirred because of them, and the women said, "Is this Naomi?"

²⁰ She said to them, "Do not call me Naomi; call me Mara, for the Almighty has dealt very bitterly with me.

[21] "I went out full, but the LORD has brought me back empty. Why do you call me Naomi, since the LORD has witnessed against me and the Almighty has afflicted me?"
[22] So Naomi returned, and with her Ruth the Moabitess, her daughter-in-law, who returned from the land of Moab. And they came to Bethlehem at the beginning of barley harvest.

A LITTLE BACKGROUND

Let's do a quick background sketch before we get too deep into this. A short historical summary will help us with our overall understanding.

The account opens in ancient Palestine in an era between Israel's conquest of the land of Canaan and the reign of the great kings, Saul, David and Solomon (about 1000 B.C.). Israel was in a state of geopolitical instability. It had no central governing authority, no real army, no preeminent leader and a very tenuous agrarian economy. Though it had a comprehensive religious code, it was by no means universally followed, since the twelve tribes were scattered over the north and south of Palestine as well as east and west of the Jordan River. Israel's cultural glue was very elastic and Scripture informs us that as a result, "everyone did what was right in his own eyes" (Judges 21:25). In other words, spiritual relativism and cultural tolerance were the accepted norms. Sounds a little like our world as we begin this third millennium A.D., doesn't it? Equally important, externally, is the fact that Israel was hated by the nations that shared her borders. As a result, she was subject to constant invasion from this host of adversarial neighbors who surrounded her.

So this was a time of socioeconomic instability and spiritual stagnation for "these people of God" who were benefactors of God's law, redemp-tion and covenant promises (Romans 9:4). But for now, due because of the instability, they were adrift in a sea of insecurity and self-centeredness. So as this account opens, this is a chaotic time in Israel.

On top of all the challenges facing these people, economic catastrophe struck. "Now it came about in the days when the judges governed, that there was a famine in the land" (Ruth 1:1). God, as promised if their behavior warranted correction, allowed a famine to decimate Israel's agricultural production (see Deuteronomy 28:12, 24). The people were left to respond to this unexpected event by making some critical lifestyle choices.

THE ISSUE: Needing Money or Needing Faith?

Economic hardship can drive a man crazy with worry and make him view his options through the distorted lenses of fear, frustration and embarrassment. If he doesn't clarify his perspective with some solid guidance from informed counselors, he is apt to make a bad situation worse. That is just what Elimelech did. Despite the unwavering counsel of God's word and the historical precedent of his forefather and patriarch Abraham (Genesis 12:10), when the drought hit, Elimelech left town and put a stake down in the land of one of Israel's neighboring pagan nations, Moab.

A drought was no real reason to leave the province of God. Men of God had previously used economic privation, as already mentioned, as a justification for moving beyond the land of God's provision to the territory of self-determination. But as before, it was always met with God's disapproval. Inevitably further problems would surface that only exacerbated the challenges the AWOL believer faced. Though the escalation of problems was regrettable, it was necessary as God's means to underscore his discipline, capture their attention and motivate them to return to their stewardship in obedience to his authority.

That was the case with Abraham (Genesis 12), Lot (Genesis 13) and other migrating men of God. The worst problem, however, was the danger their social withdrawal and economic capitulation precipitated for the family unit. Again, Abraham's example is illustrative (Genesis 12:11-20; 26:6-10). His evacuation from the territory God had assigned him nearly cost him his wife and the fulfillment of the covenant promises he received from God.

We twenty-first-century moderns may find this hard to understand. After all, today we have freedom of movement geographically and professionally. But God gave Israel covenant promises that stipulated that they were to stay in the land of his promise in order to secure his blessing and fulfill their stewardship to be his representatives to the world (Genesis 12:1-3; Exodus 19:5-6; Isaiah 49:6). Any movement away from the land was essentially a movement away from God's umbrella of fatherly-shepherding provision and protection. It was viewed as an act of defiance—*an act that lacked faith*—if an Israelite ignored the covenant and moved out of their national boundaries without God's express leading.

Israelites were also expressly prohibited from marrying foreigners, that is, people of a different religious persuasion (see Deuteronomy 7:1-13). Intermarriage with foreigners would amalgamate the religious convictions of the people, thereby diluting or corrupting Israel's unique identity as representatives to the world of this holy but gracious God.

So if orthodox Israelites wanted to enjoy the blessings of God, they needed to follow the covenant stipulations of geographical residence and spousal selection within the nation. If a person chose evacuation or intermarriage, then they were essentially choosing divine discipline. Therefore Elimelech's departure was a harbinger of bad things to come. Unfortunately for Elimelech and his family, they came quickly.

LOUSY CHOICES, LOUSY CONSEQUENCES

Elimelech had a wife, Naomi, and two sons, Mahlon and Chilion. Sometime after their arrival in Moab, Elimelech died. His sons, now adults and responsible to take up Elimelech's role as head of the family, chose wives for themselves from the pool of available women, all of whom were pagan Moabites. Both took a Moabite woman as a wife. That guaranteed that the family problems would continue. And they did!

Within ten short years, both Mahlon and Chilion were also dead, leaving behind three widows with no means of economic support nor progeny to continue the clan history and family viability. These women were now up to their necks in serious trouble.

The ancient world had no social security system as we know it for people in distress.[1] There were no life insurance companies to provide death benefits to survivors. The only economic provision was your family's inheritance or estate and income generated by healthy males. Women had few options for wage-earning work and found it hard to survive financially without a husband or son's economic provision.

The stage is set for disaster, and it comes with a vengeance. All the males are deceased, leaving three widows with no male heirs to count on for future economic viability. Because the women took on their husbands' identities, they now had no place to belong. The Israelite Naomi is geographically separated from her clan and culture, and the Moabites Ruth and Orpah are alienated from their family clans as a result of their marriages. What are these three desperate women to do?

AN IMPORTANT QUESTION

Let's first ask another question. Where did Elimelech go wrong?

No man in his right mind would purposely destroy himself, his family and his economic resources to leave his wife destitute, right? But many a man has shipwrecked his life on the shoals of disaster by making quick, economically motivated decisions during a time of financial duress.

Some men, like the greedy businesspeople of our failed American corporations, make stupid financial decisions during times of prosperity. In the late 1990s, despite enormous price-to-earning ratios[2] and personal investment portfolios growing with unusual ease, these men were not satisfied with the riches they accumulated from their salary, stock options and other benefits. They wanted more and sought to find it by hiding debt and erroneously reporting earnings. Then it all went bust. Pandora's box was opened and a cascade of corporations failed with federal investigators hot in pursuit. Who would want to be a part of that?

But more common and perhaps more tragic are those who lose faith in the face of financial crisis. Rather than persevering through a lean time, we make an irrevocable career decision in order to better provide for our family—or so we think—only to see the decision implode through unforeseen negative circumstances. The fact is, if you stray outside of God's ordained territory for you or make decisions strictly on financial considerations, you are bound for trouble.

I know; I've done it. I thought I was well balanced in my motivations when I quit one job to go to another, which required a cross-country move. But I didn't calculate the wear and tear on my family that the move would exact. I wish I would have known then what I've learned since: moving is hard on everyone. It is a traumatic experience that especially affects wives and children. Susan Miller offers insightful comments on the impact of moving in *After the Boxes Are Unpacked*, starting with a quotation of writer Audrey T. McCollum:

Leaving behind . . . whatever embodies special memories and experiences can feel like an amputation. It is the loss of a segment of family continuity, of personal history, the loss of a fragment of self.
Women . . . have an overwhelming need for a sense of belonging, a sense of community. . . . The pain of separation and the feeling of rootlessness often leaves *them* feeling wounded, affecting *their* ability to start over.
Moving is difficult for children because it involves the loss of friends, school, and the familiar things that are a part of their everyday life. . . . Toddlers will mourn the loss of their room and of the house they've always lived in. School age children will mourn the loss of their friends and the loss of their school. Teenagers, along with mourning all of the above, are likely to feel anger at their parents for a major life change that is beyond their control. Many times the move is harder for teens than for younger children.[3]

I didn't calculate how much furniture gets scratched and marred in a transcontinental move. I didn't calculate how deep our roots were in the town we had lived in for over eighteen years and how hard emotionally it would be on the family to "re-pot" in a new city. I didn't calculate how hard it would be to find new doctors, auto mechanics or a new church. I didn't calculate how hard it would be to make new friends. I didn't calculate how it would fracture our sense of community. Because I didn't calculate these things properly, only viewing the bottom line to this decision from my career's perspective, family fun dropped as low as a share of a bankrupt company's stock.

Guys, learn from me. Please think things through thoroughly before making any major professional, geographic or financial move. Pulling up roots to move to the next new thing always takes a toll. Because we are responsible for our family's welfare, we must be sure the move is worth it. We must count up all the costs. And we need to get wise counsel from those who are older and wiser. They can help us see what we are too young, inexperienced or excited now to see.

I learned the hard way that things change within a family as life progresses. Most of this evolution is so slow that it is imperceptible. As children grow their needs change more significantly than their physical growth and appearance may indicate. What worked for you right after college or in the first year of your marriage won't necessarily work years later. You may find that the rules change, that your family's basic needs are different five, ten and twenty years into marriage.

Also, a man would do well to consider the limitations of his calling. No man can do it all, have it all, be it all and change whatever he pleases with a guarantee that his game will continue to succeed (James 4:13-17). Each of us has physical, emotional and financial limitations, not to mention the limit of the lifespan itself. I am convinced that God has called each of us to be stewards of a specific territory, including our health, education, talents, family and networks. Get outside of that "ordination" and you are very likely to find yourself in over your head.

By ordination I mean God's unique gift to you personally of what he has asked you specifically to do in life. That gift contains the opportunity, experience, training, relationships and other internal and external assets that enable you to fulfill a specific stewardship domain. This is not a huge mystery. God didn't intend for it to be kept a secret from you. He wants you to know his general guidelines for your adult life as much as you would like to. Within the freedom he provides each of us we have the thrill of seeing his direction unfold as we cooperate with his leadership and yield to his Spirit's guidance.[4]

Most of us walk into our stewardship unconsciously and discover our ordination years after we've been engaged in it, taking our cues partially from successes we've seen as a result of performing out of our talents and desires. It happens that way not because we are lucky but because God's providence guides us into it. But some who thoughtfully consider their cluster of gifts, resources, circumstances and available opportunities wisely view the landscape of their life and prayerfully seek discernment. Those who do will discover a deeper and more confident sense of their arena. They are more able to assert themselves vocationally with less anxiety and a greater sense of mission.[5]

MISSING THE MARK OF MANHOOD

So what did Elimelech do wrong? Well, what he did right was to see himself as a *provider*. He just didn't get God's direction on where or how to do it. I don't pick up on one note of prayer in this narrative. In fact, he moved against all the information available to him. He choose to ignore history, the plain teaching of his Scriptures, the needs of his greater community and the cohesive relationships that enable families to succeed despite trial. In the final analysis he lost it all.

Like many of us, he also thought the sum total of his role as provider was financial. How very wrong he was. It seems he lost sight of the fact that providing for a family also involves their spiritual welfare, which we might call *pastoring*. Ignoring that, he moved his family into a pagan, forbidden environment. This led his sons to adopt the culture's values and marry pagan women.

Furthermore, he thought little of the future, only the here and now, thereby failing in his responsibility to *protect* his family. Not only did he ignore the future consequences of his decisions spiritually, culturally and relationally, he had no thought of providing for his family in the event of a catastrophic injury or untimely death.

Finally, he failed to consider the significance of social networks and a sense of community connection needed for emotional well-being. In his flight from Israel, he ignored his family's need for a sense of historical continuity. The first chapter of Ruth implies that there was no communication with the people back home during their ten-year sojourn in Moab (Ruth 1:19), causing total isolation from their roots and a sense of lost tribal or national identity. The result was that he forfeited any opportunity he had to act as a clan leader or *patriarch* to his immediate or extended family.

In later chapters we'll explore positive examples of these roles in contrast to Elimelech's failures. Interestingly Naomi, the wife of this poor example of a marital leader, had a much better grasp on the fundamental responsibility of a provider. Once the supports were knocked out of her after the death of her sons, the final leaders of her little clan, she had no further cultural obligation to stay in Moab. So she immediately planned her departure from Moab and returned to kin and kindred in Israel. And she executed her plan soon after.[6]

GETTING BACK TO THE RIGHT PLACE

One further note, men. Two words from chapter one stand out to give us insight into the needs of our wives and other women in our communities. Naomi wanted to *"return"* (Ruth 1:6, 7, 10, 11, 12, 15, 20), because she wanted *"rest"* (see 3:1).

The word *rest* carries the idea of security, a safe place wherein she can effectively fulfill her calling to conceive, bear, raise and release the next generation. But she needs an overriding protector to do that (see 2:12).

And the word *return* carries with it the idea of repentance, which brings hope to any of us who have strayed from our God-ordained place of operation and experienced the withdrawal of his favor and blessing. To repent, "to return," means simply to change our direction from going our stubborn way to going God's. We leave disobedience and turn back to him in full pursuit of faithfulness. And it begins with a change of mind.

Sometimes it takes a total disaster to get our attention. Sometimes not. Whatever the case, if you sense that you have underperformed in your responsibility to provide for your family, then for heaven's sake, and theirs, get with it. Repent—return to God's way of living.

Talk to God and ask for confirmation of your career direction. Ask him about your spiritual provision for the family. Seek his help to understand their emotional and relational needs. Also, don't discount the benefits of the familiar, of friends and family, of your networks of doctors, mechanics, lawyers and soccer coaches.

Sometimes God calls a man to unmoor his boat from the harbor of the familiar and set out into the horizon of a God-directed adventure. But more times then not, men seek adventure for adventure's sake without determining if the motivation is from the Spirit or simply from our human nature. We act out of human impulse instead of inspiration from God. When that happens we strike out because we sense our intrinsic design to initiate, penetrate and pioneer our environment but have an unclear target and even foggier spiritual justification. Without God's clear counsel, any effort to assert yourself will go unblessed, unrewarded and thwarted by our heavenly assignment giver and covenant keeper—the living God!

So explore the domain of your stewardship prayerfully, circumspectly, with godly counsel and appreciating the input of your spouse. Then pursue *provision* with all your energy in a biblically balanced effort, seeking both the health and welfare of your clan today as well as their potential needs for the future. As you do this you will ensure a life that is lived without regret.

Elimelech not only failed his stewardship miserably, but his account has been published for us all to read and evaluate. I don't envy his reputation. I am glad our failures to date haven't been published for the world to scrutinize—aren't you?

At any rate, the next guy I want to introduce you to has a much more successful and inspiring story. In fact, it both starts and ends well. For that reason I am glad Boaz's testimony has been published. I need a positive role model to show me the way of real masculinity. So without further delay, let's turn the page and get acquainted with the book's hero. In the process we'll discover how a real man succeeds in the context of his world, his community and culture.

CHAPTER 4

A REAL MAN IS A PASTOR

Ruth 2

Real heroes, as I have already mentioned, are few and far between today. Today we have celebrities—"stars." Culture is enamored with men and women of fame and fortune, people who are frontrunners in business, athletics, arts and entertainment or politics. But many fall by the wayside when the glare of public scrutiny unveils their secret sins. The 1919 "Black Sox," Ivan Boesky and Michael Milken of the '80s, the Clintons in the '90s and now Enron's Jeffrey Skilling in this new millennium. The names change but the incriminating escapades don't. They are culture's icons one day and under investigation the next. So our stars lose their luster and our celebrity heroes return to the mortal world of humans. Only something is missing. If they haven't lost our respect or trust by now they have at least lost our sympathy and our emulation.

This generation has made fun of the traditional but dependable, boring but responsible characters of yesteryear, like Jim Anderson of *Father Knows Best* acclaim. Too bad. We could use a few more Mr. Andersons today, men who are reliable, dependable, trustworthy, wise and kind. They were on the job providing for their families, and at home they were leading the clan with their steady presence, sage advice, faithful confidence and unyielding commitment to doing things right and for the right reasons.

Today with so many absentee dads and divorced dads and busy dads and bad dads,[1] it is easy to dismiss all men as irresponsible, self-consumed, aging adolescents who, like Peter Pan, have never really grown up and don't care to. But that is unfair. Most men I meet are responsible. Most want to succeed at the very things we have been discussing—being successful leaders at home, at work and in their community. Most men are stable in their careers, provide amply for their families, are faithful to their wives and attentive to their children. They mow the lawn, change the oil in the cars, paint the house, move the furniture when needed and spend their vacations going where their wife and kids want to go. We only fantasize about taking a vacation with just the boys as Billy Crystal immortalized in the popular movie *City Slickers*.

We need to cut guys some slack. They have a lot on their plate, and some are confused about their roles. That is to be expected with so many discordant voices in society proclaiming a wide variety of expectations and vying for allegiance. Add career pressure, marriage pressure, child-rearing pressure and an aging body, and it is easy for guys to take the low road of least resistance. Many give just a little of themselves to everything, leaving the rest to vegetate on the couch watching college basketball or professional golf, where they can catch a good snooze.

But it is still inspiring to watch someone who is really, really good at what they do. We appreciate extraordinary performances by celebrities who, upon achieving the inconceivable victory or impossible accomplishment, are then elevated further in our status to the station of superstar. Those who are a significant cut above the average give us a higher target, beyond mere mediocrity, for us to aim. We resonate with the idea of improving our game as we copy their techniques. And the vision their success gives us for personal improvement is a constructive motivator.

That is why Tiger Woods has captured the attention of the world's golfers, pros and wannabes alike. No matter who is leading the tournament going into Saturday, Tiger is in the hunt. And when he is leading? Forget it! He has won twenty-four of twenty-six times when leading a tournament after fifty-four holes.

Tiger's résumé is certainly enough to inspire even the most nominal golf fan. He has won thirty-nine times for a total purse of over thirty-nine million dollars. And he is only twenty-six years old! With eight victories in the majors he is well on his way to closing in on Jack Nicklaus's record of eighteen. Who knows, he may even "lap him" a time or two before his career is over. Speaking of the "golden bear," Nicklaus used to own the Master's Tournament. Not anymore. Tiger became the youngest to win it in 1997 at age twenty-one when he also set the course tournament record (18 under par 270) and produced the largest winning margin at twelve strokes better than his nearest competitor. And he has won it two times since. Man, now there is a guy to copy when it comes to performance on the links.[2]

Men who do their jobs really well are fun to watch. They also provide a wealth of solid instruction. They inspire us to greater achievement as well.

Boaz is just one such performer. In Ruth 2 we will see him in a major tournament performance of sorts. He isn't hitting little white balls on a golf course and trying to stay focused despite the gallery. But by any standard of society, then or now, he puts on a command performance, leaving every competitor in his wake, as he goes the extra mile to serve a helpless and vulnerable woman.

And he does it with the nobility of a champion.

In the accomplishment, Boaz will demonstrate, in practical fashion, the four hallmarks of manhood. His champion caliber becomes obvious in the four arenas of our stewardship responsibility, those critical roles of provider, pastor, protector and eventually a patriarch.

Ruth 2

[1] Now Naomi had a kinsman of her husband, a man of great wealth, of the family of Elimelech, whose name was Boaz.
[2] And Ruth the Moabitess said to Naomi, "Please let me go to the field and glean among the ears of grain after one in whose sight I may find favor." And she said to her, "Go, my daughter."
[3] So she departed and went and gleaned in the field after the reapers; and she happened to come to the portion of the field belonging to Boaz, who was of the family of Elimelech.
[4] Now behold, Boaz came from Bethlehem and said to the reapers, "May the LORD be with you." And they said to him, "May the LORD bless you."
[5] Then Boaz said to his servant who was in charge of the reapers, "Whose young woman is this?"
[6] The servant in charge of the reapers replied, "She is the young Moabite woman who returned with Naomi from the land of Moab.
[7] "And she said, 'Please let me glean and gather after the reapers among the sheaves.' Thus she came and has remained from the morning until now; she has been sitting in the house for a little while."
[8] Then Boaz said to Ruth, "Listen carefully, my daughter. Do not go to glean in another field; furthermore, do not go on from

this one, but stay here with my maids.

⁹ "Let your eyes be on the field which they reap, and go after them. Indeed, I have commanded the servants not to touch you. When you are thirsty, go to the water jars and drink from what the servants draw."

¹⁰ Then she fell on her face, bowing to the ground and said to him, "Why have I found favor in your sight that you should take notice of me, since I am a foreigner?"

¹¹ Boaz replied to her, "All that you have done for your mother-in-law after the death of your husband has been fully reported to me, and how you left your father and your mother and the land of your birth, and came to a people that you did not previously know.

¹² "May the LORD reward your work, and your wages be full from the LORD, the God of Israel, under whose wings you have come to seek refuge."

¹³ Then she said, "I have found favor in your sight, my lord, for you have comforted me and indeed have spoken kindly to your maidservant, though I am not like one of your maidservants."

¹⁴ At mealtime Boaz said to her, "Come here, that you may eat of the bread and dip your piece of bread in the vinegar." So she sat beside the reapers; and he served her roasted grain, and she ate and was satisfied and had some left.

¹⁵ When she rose to glean, Boaz commanded his servants, saying, "Let her glean even among the sheaves, and do not insult her.

¹⁶ "Also you shall purposely pull out for her some grain from the bundles and leave it that she may glean, and do not rebuke her."

¹⁷ So she gleaned in the field until evening. Then she beat out what she had gleaned, and it was about an ephah of barley.

[18] She took it up and went into the city, and her mother-in-law saw what she had gleaned. She also took it out and gave Naomi what she had left after she was satisfied.
[19] Her mother-in-law then said to her, "Where did you glean today and where did you work? May he who took notice of you be blessed." So she told her mother-in-law with whom she had worked and said, "The name of the man with whom I worked today is Boaz."
[20] Naomi said to her daughter-in-law, "May he be blessed of the LORD who has not withdrawn his kindness to the living and to the dead." Again Naomi said to her, "The man is our relative, he is one of our closest relatives."
[21] Then Ruth the Moabitess said, "Furthermore, he said to me, 'You should stay close to my servants until they have finished all my harvest.'"
[22] Naomi said to Ruth her daughter-in-law, "It is good, my daughter, that you go out with his maids, so that others do not fall upon you in another field."
[23] So she stayed close by the maids of Boaz in order to glean until the end of the barley harvest and the wheat harvest. And she lived with her mother-in-law.

BOAZ, A MAN OF HONOR

Let's take a brief look at the facts. First, Boaz was a great man in every sense of the word. In fact the name "Boaz" means "in him is strength," and he is described in the first verse as "a man of great wealth." The Hebrew phrase used in that verse, *gibbor hayil*, means "a man of standing," literally "a mighty man of valor, a mighty warrior, capable, efficient, worthy in battle."[3] He will prove this reputation in the next three chapters. Wow, this guy is a regular stud. He seems to excel in everything, including being tough! He's the grand slam champ of his association.

Obviously he knew how to use his gifts. He developed a successful business, accumulated great wealth, employed people to farm his land and he developed excellent relationships of mutual respect with his employees as well as the rest of his community (see Ruth 2:1-7, 14-16).

But that isn't all. Boaz used his standing simply but effectively to communicate God's blessings to others. In other words, though a businessman, a member of the laity and not a priest, he nevertheless made a point to verbalize a clear expression of his faith to the employees. And he matched his words with action, operating according to the precepts of his religion (Ruth 2:3, 4). Furthermore, and more exciting yet, is that Boaz's operational behavior as a businessman extended beyond the letter of the law (Leviticus 19:14; 23:22) to the spirit of the Lawgiver. Boaz understood God's sovereignty and superintendence. Furthermore he acknowledged those who also sought life under God's care. "May the LORD reward your work, and your wages be full from the LORD, the God of Israel, under whose wings you have come to seek refuge" (Ruth 2:12).

As a result Boaz was merciful, generous and protective. In fact, notice his response to Ruth's presence in his fields in Ruth 2:8-16, 22. Hebrew law decreed that a farm owner allow the poor to pick up the gleanings (the leftovers) after the paid harvesters had passed through the fields as a sort of social security/socioeconomic safety net for the poor. But Boaz went beyond the law's provisions to permit Ruth to glean freely in a safe and abundant environment—emotionally (2:10-11), spiritually (2:12), economically (2:14-16) and socially (2:16). He provided, protected and he pastored. His ministry to the impoverished widow was appreciated by a woman accustomed to the failures of irresponsible men and societies who overlooked the needy, as she had seen in Naomi's situation (2:19).

All of this sets up the last two chapters of the book, where Boaz reaches the pinnacle of his status as a mighty man of honor. There he develops both a romantic attachment to this woman and seeks her economic and familial security by executing the legal apparatus of a "kinsman redeemer." He then initiates the fourth and highest role of a man, a patriarch, but we'll get to that in a moment. First let's ask and answer some questions.

WHAT WOMEN WANT

Ever thought about the kind of man a woman is looking for? Strong, handsome, witty and sexy, or something along those lines, right? But this chapter doesn't support that kind of conclusion, at least not at this stage of the relationship.

So let's ask the question this way. What in a man gets a woman's attention? I am assuming that most men reading this book are dating, engaged, married or seeking remarriage. I am generalizing, but I assume that the male mating hunt will narrow down to a relationship with one special woman, typically leading to marriage and then to the procreation of one or more children. After all, that is part of our original design and God's intent since his first commission to the human race given way back in Genesis 1:28. Furthermore we are told that one purpose for the creation of a wife for the first man, Adam, was to help relieve his loneliness and isolation (Genesis 2:18ff.).

So with this assumption that marriage is likely to be part of the male experience, I am saying that manhood, when lived responsibly, will for married males involve a faithful expression of providing, pastoring and protecting his wife, children and, later, his extended family and greater community. And it all begins with that one special woman.

So back to the question. What in a man gets a woman's attention? Certainly wealth doesn't hurt (2:1). But character eclipses wealth. Though a woman may be impressed with a man's money, if it is not linked to character she will soon grow suspect of his faithfulness and whether he can be trusted to protect her and her children. William Harley in his classic book *His Needs, Her Needs* makes the statement that in twenty-five years of counseling he observes that marriages fail because of two things, "lack of honesty and lack of cooperation"— not, as I once thought, a lack of money.[4]

Another attribute women prefer in men is kindness accompanied by spiritual sincerity (Ruth 2:4, 9-12). The prevailing image of a tough guy today doesn't include this attribute—only "wussies" are tender. And spiritual interest is just for women and children, right? Not so. Stu Weber makes an important distinction when he writes,

> We want tender warriors . . . not soft males. *Webster's Dictionary* nicely distinguishes between the terms. Tender is linked to the Latin root, *tendre*, which means "to stretch out, or extend." The word itself is defined as "expressing or expressive of feelings of love, compassion, kindness; affectionate, as in a tender caress; considerate; careful."
>
> In contrast, when the word "soft" is used to describe an individual, it means "mild, effeminate, easily yielding to physical pressure; . . . untrained for hardship."[5]

So a real man must be tender at times, especially when he is dealing with the weak and helpless, and certainly tough and trained for hardship at other times, when dealing with enemies, adversaries and opponents to his success.

By the way, on this issue of spirituality, a psychologist friend of mine, Steve Green, tells me that a spiritual man, one who exudes quiet confidence, sincere gentleness and an unashamed purity, is highly attractive to a woman—so much so that he cautions such men of integrity to be careful of a women's receptivity to his innocent courtesies. Sometimes their attraction to the spiritual in a man can lead rather quickly to an emotional and physical attraction as well. That can quickly lead you both into compromise. Perhaps that's one reason so many ministers fall to infidelity. At any rate, spiritual development is yet another asset a male has at his disposal for success in this life.

Finally, there is an additional cluster of preferences woman look for in men. They seek those who show genuine appreciation for their contributions. They desire men who are concerned for their welfare and attentive to their needs. They desire and deserve to be respected for their humanity. And most women love unexpected gifts (Ruth 2:16). All of these Boaz graciously extended to Ruth without ever once making her feel patronized or depreciated. In fact, he extended these courtesies with honor.

Now, these may not seem like the attributes of a "valiant warrior" by modern standards, but they are by God's. Certainly they represent the chivalry of a bygone era. And the results? Well, first these two desperate women were rescued from the threat of starvation (2:17-19). Second, Ruth was protected from the humiliation of rape (2:22). These are remarkable achievements. It is honorable for a man to help others without any expectation of reciprocity (Luke 14:12-14). And it is the mark of sincere spirituality to help others with moral integrity (James 2:27).

However, both Boaz and Ruth are single, so the story and their budding relationship will continue. But for now, in the context of our "one woman" commitment, I think there are some legitimate lessons to learn. So let's talk.

A Real Man Is a Pastor

PEP TALK FOR MEN

Guys, let's pretend were in a locker-room environment right now. It is just us. We have a secluded place where we can debrief, congratulate or console one another after the game of life. Here we receive some much needed coaching, correction or encouragement before we reenter the fray. Since there are now no women present let's get honest about this issue, man to man. Okay?

Men, it's just us right now, so let's take some time to debunk some myths and correct some bad habits. General male performance on the field of female relationships has stunk lately. I think it's because we've been playing to the crowd of pop culture's applause instead of playing to win respect and the achievement of our God-given role.

Satan doesn't want you to feel confident and successful in your role as a male. He doesn't want you to have a satisfying relationship with your wife. He doesn't want you to have a stable environment at home with your kids. He doesn't want you to have an atmosphere of spiritual blessing at your job. He wants you to be miserable. Out of balance, overtaxed, angry, vacationless, recreationally selfish, inattentive to your kids, insensitive to your wife and overbearing at work. Or perhaps overdrinking, overeating, undersleeping and underexercised. In other words he wants you to be a wreck. He has a thousand strategies to get you off God's target and on his. And we play into Satan's game plan by our ignorance, selfishness, distraction, laziness or willful rebellion.

It's time to stop playing badly, go back to the fundamentals and discipline ourselves to do this right. With practice we will get better.

Of course we will never be perfect, but what a joy it would be to reverse the tide of defeated and despairing marriages with distracted and deviating husbands. Let's see the gleam return to our wives' eyes as they feel appreciated again—protected, provided for and pastored. In other words, treat them like we care, like we once told them when we talked them into an engagement!

That is the game we are in—to bring stability to our world, starting with a stable, secure family.

This won't happen without a heavenly perspective being applied horizontally to our everyday world. We need to return to faith in the God who created us and called us to live responsibly before him in the world he's entrusted to us—problems, challenges and all. We need a faith that cares about people, that wants to see their lives blessed. We need a faith that works hard, knowing that our opportunities and resources are a stewardship from God.

We need a faith that provides adequately for those we employ and leaves extra for those who have critical needs. We need a faith that stimulates us to excel in our marketplace and a faith that demands integrity as a foundation for excellence. And we need a faith that engenders love. A love for all just as God loves us (John 13:34) and held nothing back in his effort to retrieve us from sin and its resulting separation, in order to reconnect us in healthy fellowship within his family—all by the redemptive death of his Son (Ephesians 5:25).

We need this faith because without it, not only can we never succeed in the individual stewardship God has set before us, we can't even see it. We can't imagine it!

IMAGINE THIS

Imagine . . .

Imagine a world without divorce, where two people meet, fall in love, commit to a lifetime of mutual giving and support and complete their lives together.

Imagine a world where children can depend upon their fathers to make career decisions that have their best interests as paramount and not his career advancement alone.

A Real Man Is a Pastor

Imagine a world of purity, with no more premarital sex, extramarital affairs, sexually transmitted diseases, prostitution, homosexuality, sexual abuse or pornography, but instead a world of genuine love without illicit, erotic or prurient intentions.

Imagine a world where work works, where people are satisfied with their assignment, appreciated by those who lead them and in return respect those who lead. Imagine a job where everyone makes enough and then a little more than expected. Imagine a work environment where no one complains, compares, competes or criticizes.

Imagine a world where neighbors take care of each other—so well, in fact, that welfare, social security and begging are completely unnecessary.

Imagine a world where peace and prosperity are commonplace.

What you are imaging is the world the psalmist calls *shalom and shalvah* (Psalm 122:7), peace and prosperity. It is the desire each one of God's people has in their hearts because he placed it there. In fact, that is the world God desired for his people Israel. He even tried to set them up for success by providing them with their own nation, moral/legislative system, spiritual guidelines and religious professionals whose sole job was to ensure the moral integrity and thereby the social, familial, economic and vocational blessing of the populace (Deuteronomy 28:1-14). Israel was even given special judges to help lead them civically in order to further ensure progress in regard to a blessed life.

So this imagining isn't foolhardy dreaming. It is what we were created for and redeemed for, and what we have forsaken because of a lack of personal faith and fortitude. But Boaz brings these incredible concepts to fruition, by living a life of steadfast love for God and his program of goodness and grace for his people. Boaz's life shows us how to move from theology and theory to practice and impact.

What do you think? Ridiculous? Am I imagining the seemingly impossible? This side of heaven, yes, if the dream is to be fulfilled in its entirety. But it is not unimaginable if we believe God wants us to live on a higher plane of social intercourse and personal success in our day-to-day lives.

Do you think we have to have the divorces, abuse and social problems that are escalating and plaguing our communities today? Is that what God wants for us? Is that the best we can do in cooperation with his infinite power? Of course not! We are just not imagining anything better for ourselves, our families or our communities than the status quo.

We are letting Satan's deceptions and the degeneration of society lower our sense of spiritual expectation for ourselves and for our world. It's time to turn the tide, time to improve our golf score, if you will.

So where is the practical, potential high-water mark of reality in this dream that I imagine? That is up to you and me. It will be according to the measure of our faith. We are responsible to do the best we can by his grace coursing through our lives. The outcomes for faithfulness are God's responsibility. Our responsibility is the process. His responsibility is the final outcome. We can't control results; we can only control our effort. We are just under obligation to do our part. The problem is most of us have left our part to others in society and then wonder why God doesn't do something. It's because we have forgotten what it is like to be "valiant men, mighty warriors, great, wealthy leaders" for our families and communities as God's men. Simple, nondescript men like farmer Boaz! But powerful enough to affect whole communities and preserve both family and nation.

Enough locker-room talk for today. It's time for practice, time to hit our world running. But don't forget the fundamentals. Practice doesn't make perfect, practice makes permanent! That is why it is imperative to practice the right things, the things God has revealed for us in Scripture.

So let's review the game plan. Remember, the goal is to live responsibly. That defines manhood. Responsibility is to be worked out, through our conduct, in the context of community—home and neighborhood. The fundamental ingredient that will help us use the right techniques in these areas is faith.

And the object of our faith is in God through his Son, our Savior Jesus Christ. Our faith will include submission to God's performance guidelines found in the course layout, Scripture. Plus we have his guarantee to be with us, enabling us to succeed. That is a promise for a partnership greater than any caddie's.

All of this provides the confidence we need to take our positions on the field of battle, the game of life. But the illustration breaks down at this point because the stakes are too high. No mere golf game compares with the health and welfare of our wives, children and neighbors.

This contest isn't about golf, this is about souls—your soul and mine and the souls of those we love, our community and nation. Guys, it's time to improve our game. Now!

CHAPTER 5

A REAL MAN IS A PROTECTOR

Ruth 3

According to legend, King Arthur dreamed of a glorious kingdom with boundless prosperity and populated by a people of virtue. His dream was nearly achieved. His reign of nobility found its strength through the character of his attending knights. These valiant and chivalrous men fought beside him and helped him rule his realm from the round table of regal authority. But despite the kingdom's ultimate victory over the dark forces of the Mordred, the wonderful vision of Camelot was ultimately capsized, sunk by the infidelity of his best knight, Sir Lancelot, and the king's beautiful wife, Guinevere. Their romance was a sordid affair that tarnished the reputation of the king's knights, thereby soiling the highest ideals of society—virtue, trust, loyalty and commitment. In the end, Camelot fell short of Arthur's dream.

These kinds of stories always bug me. I've grown impatient with the world's perspective that seems to extol a sense of romance over responsibility. These stories are so captivating, the characters so riveting, their circumstances so understandable that we soon sympathize with their justifications of misconduct and condone their misbehavior. *After all,* we think, *they were so in love, and the king was so* much older than she was. *It was a marriage of responsibility, not romance. She never really loved him.* At least that is how the justification seems to go in the world of art and entertainment.

Maybe it's true. Maybe these stories really do represent the practical reality of life, that beautiful women fall romantically for handsome, dashing men despite the dignity, power, prestige and integrity of their husbands. And so affairs happen.

But what about some dignity? Where did duty run off to? Where are the stories of good people who do great things despite the pressure and permission that their hormones and a promiscuous culture give them? Is anybody faithful, pure and noble? Can a story have a happy, virtuous ending, or do intrigue and infidelity have to dominate every drama, imagined or real?

MEN'S NEEDS, WOMEN'S NEEDS

Let me stop the tirade there and ask a question. What do most women want in a relationship with a man? Sex? Romance? Endless revenue streams?

Not from what I read and observe. It seems to me that what most women want in a marriage is *security*. That catches most men by surprise. Why? Men are wired differently from women, as many marriage books tell us and observation reinforces.

Yet men are single-minded when they consider how to penetrate their world as they pursue success. Men think that our way, the way we're wired, is the only way to view the variables of life. As a result, we often overlook what women think and what they need. As one author says,

> Without the awareness that we are supposed to be different, men and women are at odds with each other. We usually be-

come angry or frustrated with the opposite sex because we have forgotten this important truth. We expect the opposite sex to be more like ourselves. We desire them to "want what we want and feel the way we feel." . . . Men mistakenly expect women to think, communicate, and react the way we do; women mistakenly expect men to feel, communicate and respond the way women do. We have forgotten that men and women are supposed to be different. As a result our relationships are filled with unnecessary friction and conflict.[1]

Likewise, another author writes:

Obviously the way to keep a husband and wife happily married is for each of them to meet the needs that are most important to the other. . . . I discovered why that is such a difficult assignment. Nearly every time I asked couples to list their needs according to their priority, men listed them one way and women the opposite way. Of the ten basic emotional needs, the five listed as most important by men were usually the five least important for the women and vice versa.[2]

I've had some fun through the years trying to define this issue and simplify it for myself as a tool for my ministry. Brenda, my wife, and I have conducted pastoral marriage counseling for couples who have been a part of our lives. Just to tease her, somewhere along the line I developed a short memorable acronym for defining the differences between men and women. But it stuck, because it is closer to the truth than I first imagined. I shared it with her in a sort of tongue-in-cheek manner. She laughed at first because she knew that it was my typical male attempt to keep things simple when discussing relationships. But we decided that though highly simplistic, the acronym was a fairly accurate summary of gender differences. Then she confessed that she had come to approximately the same conclusion but would not have dared to put it so succinctly.

When I talk with men and the subject of understanding women comes up, especially the theme that "we can't seem to get on the same wavelength," I tell the men to think about SARS. No, not the virus known as severe acute respiratory syndrome that has been wreaking havoc on the international health community. This SARS stands for the four separate and specific motivational needs the two genders desire in the context of relationship. For men and women these four letters represent both the critical needs as each gender defines success as well as the difference in how they prioritize them. And what is amazing is how opposite we look at the options of life.

	Men	**Women**
S	Sex	Security
A	Adventure	Affection
R	Respect	Relationship
S	Success	Stability

Men want SARS: Sex, Adventure, Respect and Success. And women want SARS too. But they seek a different set of needs: Security, Affection, Relationship and Stability.[3] So not only are the hot buttons for men and women different things, the different priorities can potentially threaten each other's achievement of these critical needs.

Men, for instance, are pretty focused on sexual pleasure and conquest. But women typically are more concerned with the security of their home and the progeny that sexual activity produces. For most men, sex is more about satisfaction—sexual satisfaction—than about security. And it doesn't take much to get our motor running. A simple glance at our wife in her nightgown and we're ready for "action." It doesn't work that way for most women. More often than not, women will feel more like enjoying a sexual experience with her man if she feels secure in the relationship and if her husband is taking the necessary steps to secure their home. If a woman is experiencing anxiety over the quality of the relationship, you can be assured that her sexual appetite will be restricted.

Second, men seek adventure as a natural expression of their role to exercise dominion over creation. Adventure includes the exploration of career options and includes penetrating into the frontiers of life with confidence and courage in the pursuit of career goals. As men seek to exploit and then develop an opportunity in order to achieve some productive net benefit, they often take great risks to do it. In fact, risk often gives men the feeling that they are really alive and gives them a sense that they are expressing their masculinity by living life to the full. There is a certain thrill in exploration and risk, and sometimes the feeling of thrill itself can become addictive. And men don't mind having fun while they pursue their conquest of the frontiers of life. That is why no self-respecting sales conference would go without a golf outing or other recreational event for the guys.

On the other hand, a man's willingness to risk, as he pursues the conquest of each successive frontier, can threaten a woman's sense of stability, either real or imagined. She may think her man is risking irresponsibly as he chases his career dream around the world. She feels no "thrill" in being dragged around the country with the family as they move from one city to another, wreaking havoc on her sense of community. Women have a tendency toward nurture, which is related to the "privilege and blessing of bearing children."[4] So it makes sense that they value an environment that enables them to succeed, and that they grow agitated when that environment is disrupted. As a woman weighs the adverse consequences on relationships, she'll typically conclude that she is experiencing unsuccessful living, despite whatever new title, responsibilities and compensation package her husband may have achieved.

Third, men are built for respect. We need to know that our humanity and our efforts are appreciated by others, especially those we seek to lead and serve. We'd exchange a good meal for respect, and many a man has exchanged a good wife for an affair because he was being fed more respect from his paramour than his wife. But to get respect from their wives men need to give them the affection they crave and deserve.

Affection is more than physical contact, though a good back rub, gentle caressing and simple handholding are a soothing potion to many women. For most females, affection means care and attention. Affection can often be measured by how well we know our wife's needs and fears. When we violate their sense of need or heighten their fear through some half-thought-through adventurous exploit, we show that we have not paid attention to them as people. They interpret the insensitivity to mean that we either don't know them very well or don't care. Ouch! We just weren't thinking the way they were. Affection begins with paying attention and includes valuing their input and feelings in making decisions. This means making joint decisions instead of you making unilateral decisions that you and your wife will both regret.

In other words, our wives are saying to us, "If you love me, you will touch me, hold me, talk to me, consider my feelings, accept my input and not abandon me for your career." This is how our wives often evaluate success in life, not by your job title or golf score!

Finally, men tend to have a bent toward vocational success. We often measure that success by title, compensation package, access to power, a position of prestige and the material emblems that prove our height on the relative ladder of success. Now, it's true that the right kinds of success can build real relational bonds between a man and a woman. This is especially true when we pursue success with a view to meeting the needs of our women.

However, career or athletic success unmitigated by wisdom, satisfaction and protection of current assets could cost a man everything. When we "roll the dice" one more time trying to double our winnings in the game of life, we can end up losing it all. Unchecked by wisdom, risk-taking can develop into compulsive gambling. I'm not talking about gaming tables, I'm talking about gambling with our career, family, health and finances. Too much risk, too many times, without substantial reason, can be our undoing.

Success accumulated God's way is a blessing to be enjoyed. But success for success's sake can be blinding. Being blinded by the pitfalls that line the road to success can jeopardize a man's health, pocketbook, sense of esteem, emotions and most importantly the stability of his wife and kids. That real or perceived threat to a woman's sense of stability can ultimately lead to divorce.

As simple as my little four-letter reminder is for the differing priorities of men and women, I find the tool helpful. It's nice to keep things simple. Sophistication has its place. But for men, keeping it simple is probably the only way we'll do well at marriage. So if my outline helps, great. Remember that the four male needs of Sex, Adventure, Respect and Success can be a threat to a female's need for Security, Affection, Relationship and Stability.

These four issues are not exhaustive explanations of male and female differences. They are generalizations intended to be a bit humorous and provide a quick summary for our understanding. The brevity also provides a little shock value—it gets people thinking,

A Real Man Is a Protector

talking and discussing. That can be a healthy exercise, especially for men. But what I am most interested in is getting men to see that we are operating on an AM frequency while our wives are tuned into FM. If we are going to lead our homes and communities successfully as providers, pastors and protectors, we need to appreciate the different needs and perspectives of others.

That is what I appreciate about our current study. In the four-chapter book of Ruth, we get a brief but fundamental review of the role of men with respect to the needs of women within the context of God's intended community.

CHIVALRY IS NOT DEAD

The matriarch of the story, Naomi, helps us to remember our responsibilities by what she is seeking for her and her daughter-in-law. In fact, we do not get far into this chapter before she reminds us of one of the critical needs for most women. Ruth 3 begins with Naomi asking Ruth, "My daughter, shall I not seek security for you, that it may be well with you?" (Ruth 3:1). See it there? It is the word *security*. It shouts for our attention. Are we listening, men?

In some order of priority we all have to deal with sex, security, adventure and affection, plus respect, relationships, success and stability. You can quibble with some of my generalizations, but I think most of us would agree that at the top of the two gender lists are two very different priorities: sex for men, security for women.

That is why Boaz remains a relevant hero to me today. This chapter sets forth a potential tension between those two great and often competing drives between the sexes. The outcome of Boaz's behavior provides us with a template for honest, healthy male-female relationships. It supports the concept of chivalry, where a noble man provides for a woman's needs in an environment of purity.[5]

ROMANCE AND RESPONSIBILITY

Remember that Naomi and Ruth are still trying to recover from total financial and familial loss. Their impoverished circumstances are the direct result of Elimelech's misdirected career decision, which resulted in the family's move to Moab.

Now back in Israel, these two economically deprived widows are seeking to meet their primary need of financial security. They were just trying to survive. They needed a job in order to eat. And because in Israel economic viability was directly linked to property ownership, which was held by men, one or the other of them needed a husband.

So Naomi goes to work crafting a strategy to lure "successful and respectable" Boaz (2:1) into a romantic encounter meant to raise his sense of desire and duty. Security is the reason they were attempting to coax Boaz into a wedding proposal. His marriage to Ruth would solve both of the women's key priorities—financial stability and family revival.

What gets my attention is how responsibly Boaz behaved when he could have taken sexual advantage of the situation—something most men would have done then and most would do today. But he didn't. Let's see if I can back up those comments from the text of Scripture.

Ruth 3

[1] Then Naomi her mother-in-law said to her, "My daughter, shall I not seek security for you, that it may be well with you?
[2] "Now is not Boaz our kinsman, with whose maids you were? Behold, he winnows barley at the threshing floor tonight.
[3] "Wash yourself therefore, and anoint yourself and put on your best clothes, and go down to the threshing floor; but do not

make yourself known to the man until he has finished eating and drinking.

⁴ "It shall be when he lies down, that you shall notice the place where he lies, and you shall go and uncover his feet and lie down; then he will tell you what you shall do."

⁵ She said to her, "All that you say I will do."

⁶ So she went down to the threshing floor and did according to all that her mother-in-law had commanded her.

⁷ When Boaz had eaten and drunk and his heart was merry, he went to lie down at the end of the heap of grain; and she came secretly, and uncovered his feet and lay down.

⁸ It happened in the middle of the night that the man was startled and bent forward; and behold, a woman was lying at his feet.

⁹ He said, "Who are you?" And she answered, "I am Ruth your maid. So spread your covering over your maid, for you are a close relative."

¹⁰ Then he said, "May you be blessed of the LORD, my daughter. You have shown your last kindness to be better than the first by not going after young men, whether poor or rich.

¹¹ "Now, my daughter, do not fear. I will do for you whatever you ask, for all my people in the city know that you are a woman of excellence.

¹² "Now it is true I am a close relative; however, there is a relative closer than I.

¹³ "Remain this night, and when morning comes, if he will redeem you, good; let him redeem you. But if he does not wish to redeem you, then I will redeem you, as the LORD lives. Lie down until morning."

¹⁴ So she lay at his feet until morning and rose before one could recognize another; and he said, "Let it not be known

that the woman came to the threshing floor."
¹⁵ Again he said, "Give me the cloak that is on you and hold it." So she held it, and he measured six measures of barley and laid it on her. Then she went into the city.
¹⁶ When she came to her mother-in-law, she said, "How did it go, my daughter?" And she told her all that the man had done for her.
¹⁷ She said, "These six measures of barley he gave to me, for he said, 'Do not go to your mother-in-law empty-handed.'"
¹⁸ Then she said, "Wait, my daughter, until you know how the matter turns out; for the man will not rest until he has settled it today."

First, observe that Boaz is in a legal position to rescue these women and the family inheritance because of his lineage relationship to the deceased. In other words Boaz could perform the levirate marriage function,[6] according to Jewish law, because he was in the same family line as Naomi's ex-husband (Deuteronomy 24:5-10). Jewish law demanded that property stay within the family for the sake of the stability of the family inheritance and their economic viability. So a widow who remarried was to be remarried within the family line of her deceased husband, if she remarried at all. And Boaz was in the same lineage of Elimelech, so he could legally fulfill the role.

Second, notice that Naomi has Ruth prep and primp herself in order to maximize her attractiveness as she presents herself to this available bachelor. No doubt Naomi's advice to "wash . . . and anoint yourself and put on your best clothes" was meant to accentuate her beauty and stimulate desire (Ruth 3:3-5).

But Naomi also had Ruth strategically position herself at Boaz's feet. Why? This was a culturally acceptable request for security through marriage. To "cover herself with his cloak by uncovering his feet" was an assertive statement of her availability without it being a misleading suggestion of sexual receptivity.[7] In other words, she didn't lay next to him or "with him" but below his feet, awakening him only after the night air chilled his feet with the removal of the covering that shielded them.

Finally, notice the respect they extended Boaz by working their plan into his normal custom without disrupting his schedule. They waited until after he "had eaten and drunk and his heart was merry" (3:7) before initiating their plan. And Ruth obediently and discreetly followed all of Naomi's advice, while maintaining the dignity for which she had become reputable (3:6-11).

But now notice Boaz. He is hard working and prosperous. He is not an absentee boss (3:2) but was on site, managing the work, assisting in the harvest. He was also fun loving and celebratory. Boaz knew how to enjoy the gifts of life that God had given him and when to do it—at harvest time, when the work was complete.

Notice too that his sense of duty governs his sense of desire (3:8-13). When Boaz finally awakens and notices the presence of this available young woman, he offers no sexual proposition. He doesn't let his libido override his integrity. He simply recognizes her request (3:9), extols her kindness and promises to respond to her invitation for an ancient Jewish levirate marriage contract.

Boaz decides to take up the challenge of family and community responsibility presented by Naomi and Ruth's plight. Because the stakes include the survival of these two precious and vulnerable lives, he vows to do all that he can to "save" them.

However, there is a caveat. There is a closer relative, someone first in line to the lineage of Elimelech. Boaz is honor-bound to inform the women that the other relative must be given the first shot at "redeeming" them. Boaz also intends to inform this other relative that Elimelech's property includes marriage to the last surviving widow of the deceased male heirs—Ruth. That is the way Jewish law read, and Boaz intended to follow it to the letter. What a man of integrity!

It is all done with honor. It is all respectful. And lest there be even the suspicion of impropriety, Boaz forfeits the pleasure of her company for the remainder of the night by sending her home before she is recognized with the approach of dawn's light. Otherwise they risked that the night's ritual might be discovered, misconstrued and misinterpreted. They knew that gossip would jeopardize both of their reputations and foil their plan for redemption before a marriage betrothal could be negotiated with the rest of Elimelech's surviving family. However, as testament to Boaz's sincerity, he did not allow her to leave without providing an enormous amount of grain that she and Naomi could use for their personal sustenance (3:14-18).

I guess most women would view this as a romantic love story, and they are probably right. But for me, I see a noble man, Boaz. Compared to the philanderers and sexual abusers that capture the imagination of our Hollywood producers and roam our corporate offices, college campuses and quiet suburban neighborhoods, I find this story inspiring and motivating.

Now let's have a private discussion again—just us, in our imaginary locker room.

STRAIGHT TALK

Guys, many of us have failed in the matter of sexual purity. We haven't always respected the dignity of the women we've dated. And some of us, frankly, have taken advantage of their vulnerability. Sometimes we've even traded sex for the promise of security. Most of us also struggle with immoral thoughts as we eye a beautiful woman. And some of us are caught in the grip of pornography as we read these words.

I am sorry.

I will let others more righteous or self-righteous than me say "shame on us." The fact is sex is a strong internal drive for men, who are naturally endowed by their creator with high-voltage testosterone. But according to Scripture sex outside of marriage is wrong. So we have to learn to control our urges and impulses.

Yet men will never learn to live nobly by being reminded of their ignobility. Men will live nobly when inspired by the practical and positive example of an exemplary model—like Boaz. And men can live up to God's ideal when they live in concert with God's Spirit, which Scripture tells us lives within each believer, providing the power we need to resist sinful impulses and temptations and enabling us to live more like Christ, in healthy purity. So we have a shot for success after all.

I am a realist. I have been around enough to know how available sex is in the office. I hear what a hidden but promiscuous environment some singles groups become even at church.[8] If any of the modern literature is true, then the so-called sexual revolution is escalating rapidly, providing even more opportunity for men to meet their sexual fantasies while abrogating their moral responsibilities.

The opportunity for immorality knows no bounds. The workplace provides one of the most common arenas for men and women to establish a close relationship, professional at first, that can escalate into emotional and then physical intimacy very quickly.

The industry that I work in, professional motor racing, is legendary for its fast men and women. They are often in and out of bed as fast as a tire changer on a Winston Cup Car! In fact the action is so common that we have a sobriquet for the young beautiful women who adorn our sport with the purpose of attaching themselves to one of the men. They are known not so affectionately as "Pit Lizards." Many single and even married men have been bitten by the reptile of illicit sexual opportunity only to see their escapade end in guilt, remorse, shame, a sexually transmitted disease, a broken marriage and in a few cases death through AIDS. Sexual sport can be as dangerous as racing.

However, just this week at one of the racetracks I witnessed a noble act by a man of honor. Gary (not his real name), a growing Christian and a young and handsome auto racing professional, pulled me aside for a conversation just before the green flag dropped. We hadn't seen each other in over a year and he wanted to bring me up to speed on some things.

As we stood next to the garage entrance a beautiful woman approached him. They obviously knew each other well and immediately struck up a fairly intense conversation as she excitedly told him all that was going on in her life. The one detail I caught was that she had been married in the past year but her husband was not with her this weekend because he was racing in another series. "During race season we only see each other twice a week," she said. I didn't think much of it at the time, and since I was getting in the way of their conversation, I excused myself and left.

Not five seconds later I felt Gary rush up beside me. "Hey, man," I said, "you don't need to hang out with me. Our conversation is over. I left because I didn't want to interrupt your reunion with Becka."

But before I could go further with my explanation, Gary interrupted. "No, Jim, you don't understand. As a single man I have no business being alone with any woman who is here this weekend without her husband. I needed to get out of that conversation!"

"Oh, Gary, I'm sorry," I apologized. "It didn't really connect that you might be in a precarious spot. I just didn't want to be dead baggage to a conversation—"

"Jim, it's okay," he interrupted again. "In fact, you did me a favor breaking off the conversation and giving me an excuse to follow after you. It is better for me to stay away, so thanks."

Wow. I wouldn't have known what his motives were for talking with her, nor what they might have done later that evening after the race was over and everyone went back to their hotel rooms. It just wasn't on my radar screen because I wasn't tuned into her. But Gary was tuned in. Gary knew something I didn't, and he dealt with it decisively. Gary did the very best thing he could by leaving, moving away from temptation and on to honor. Keeping away from even the suggestion of impropriety is a good rule of thumb for any man who wants to live life virtuously and treat women with dignity. That is a man of honor.

THE CHALLENGE

Guys, here is the deal, the real deal. We not only don't have to lower ourselves to the base desires of our sexual urges. We can soar above culture's casual indifference to sexual misconduct and initiate a whole new level of male behavior toward women.

We can treat them with respect. We can seek to meet their needs without ulterior motive. We can live nobly and treat women as Jesus did. As the apostle Paul exhorts, we can honor "the older women as mothers, and the younger women as sisters, in all purity" (1 Timothy 5:2). We can also see beyond women's physical attractiveness and, as the apostle Peter recommended, look at "the hidden person of the heart" (1 Peter 3:4).

I don't care what others are doing, how they excuse it, what justification they have. We can live above the scandals of today's sexual predators. We can harness the energy of our sexual desire. We can learn to pursue sexual gratification properly, in the bounds of a healthy marriage relationship. God's Word says we should. God's Spirit says we can. And Boaz shows us how. That is the real deal, guys. That's being a real man, God's way!

Let's see ourselves in Boaz's position, the position of a responsible male to whom others are looking to bring about a redemptive change in the lives of those who have needs. We need some more heroes. People have lost a sense of nobility because there are so few who model those characteristics. The high bar of proper behavior has been lowered so far that scalawags are role models today. We need to reverse that by following the lead of Boaz.

Here are two questions. Your answers will reveal how you view your role on the planet at this time in history. Ready? Here we go. If you are in a position of strength, do you take advantage of that position and satisfy your impulses as reward for your strength, as the spoils go to the victors? Or do you limit your self-satisfaction so that you can harness your strength for the benefit of others, especially those in a vulnerable state?

In my opinion if you answer yes to the first question you are a hedonist, no matter what your religious philosophy. But if you affirm the second question, then you are seeking to live redemptively. This suggests that you are here as God's representative. Our forebears were the first to need God's redemptive intervention way back in the garden of Eden. God had been in the redemption business ever since.

I am convinced that God is looking for noble men to join him in that practical task today. He elevates those who seek to help the dependent without taking advantage of their tenuous situation. We don't need any more exploiters. We need more redeemers.

In this culture it is almost unheard of to be a virgin until marriage. Those that make it that far are often ridiculed by their peers.[9] And in the racing community, where I minister much of the time, it is the norm for people to live together for years before they decide to commit to marriage. Why is that so?

I think it is because we have lowered the standard of what is permissible and acceptable, even what's expected. Our Hegelian moral ethic has degenerated to a norm that accepts anything as tolerable for consenting adults.[10] How else would you explain not only unmarried heterosexual partners but homosexual ones? And nobody seems to care!

Though we have lowered the standard, we can't change the inherent drive and highest priority for most women, security. Nor can we alter the priority God puts on the value of virtue (Leviticus 19:2). We can only lower our own sense of conscience and deceive ourselves into a lower standard for human relationships and sexuality.

But it doesn't have to be this way. We can stop the moral slide and start a new trend. We can raise the bar on purity again. We can reassert the chivalrous code of honor between men and the women they are called to serve, women who desire security and men who see it as a sacred trust. That is part of the "glorious realm" we have the privilege of guarding. But will we?

Men, think about this. Don't you want your sons to marry chaste women? Don't you want your daughters to date without fear of molestation? Doesn't morality matter, at least for the safety of your kids, if not for yourself?

Guys, it's imperative that we drop our self-gratifying desire for erotic stimulation in favor of the higher priority of women's desire for security and right to chastity. When we do so, then we will be males worthy of the time-honored title of men, noble men. Men who by conscience surrender our selfish drives and "buy back" (redeem) the values and virtues of a godly society as we provide security for our women, protect their vulnerable humanity and pastor them with godly leadership that seeks their best interests above ours.

That is the calling of a man, to serve his family and greater community as a virtuous provider, pastor and protector. Men, it's time once again to take the field and put our game talk into action. On this critical issue, what do you say we reassert ourselves to play God's way? It's time to play to win!

CHAPTER 6

A REAL MAN IS A PATRIARCH

Ruth 4

Dale Earnhardt was one of the greatest race car drivers that ever lived. Unlike many winners who come and go, his longevity in the sport was testament to his special abilities. When he died at age fifty in an unlikely crash during the last lap of the 2001 Daytona 500, he was not only still on top of his game, many felt that that year he would break the Winston Cup championship total he shared with "King" Richard Petty. Dale was a favorite to win an eighth championship.

His untimely death was not only a blow to that championship run. It was a devastating blow to all of racing. In one awful, unexpected moment we lost one of the sport's greatest drivers, biggest heroes, most generous citizens and toughest competitors. He was also one of the smartest, most strategic, naturally talented men to strap into a 750-horsepower stock car.

Life will never be the same in Winston Cup racing without "The Intimidator." But his racing legacy will live on through the careers of his two sons, Kerry and Dale Jr., and through the many other drivers he helped as a teacher and mentor.

Jeff Gordon, for instance, had this to say about Dale's role in his own racing career: "Brooke [Gordon] and I are deeply saddened by this devastating loss. Not only is it a huge loss for this sport, but a huge loss for me personally. Dale taught me so much and became a great friend."[1]

Steve Park, the first driver hired to race for Dale's personal racing team at Dale Earnhardt Incorporated, fondly remembers the "boss" and the special interest he took in Steve, especially the coaching Dale gave him as a driver.

> One never received a pat on the back for running second. That's just the way he taught us. If you want to call it tough love, that's the way I was brought up by my mom and dad, and that's kinda what drew me to Dale Earnhardt Inc. If you did something right, you might get one of those half smiles underneath that mustache, or if you did something wrong, you were out baling hay in the hot sun with him. It's a tough way to learn but you always remember . . . he taught us how to be winners. That is something you can't replace.[2]

Well, it is a long stretch from the 200-miles-per-hour world of professional racing to our 55-mile-per-hour lives. But if we have trouble relating to The Intimidator, let's at least consider the principles of excellence common to every competitive sport.

In racing it's a combination of speed, balance, timing, trust, assertion and confidence all within the context of a well-oiled team where communication is essential. In football agility, stamina, strength, position and drive are other well-known fundamentals, discipline being a hallmark. Baseball, tennis, surfing, golf and so on all have their fundamentals too. But what the sporting world celebrates the most are the champions. They are the athletes who have mastered the basics and exceed them in performance. They are a cut above their peers. In any sport there are basic methods and techniques that have to be learned if one intends to succeed. Each contestant must not only know but must master the fundamentals if they want to be a success. These fundamentals, well performed, become the foundation that superstars build upon as they exhibit their exceptional talent. The combination of flawless fundamentals coupled with consistent, extraordinary performances are the hallmarks of true champions.

Each sport typically awards its best performers at the end of the year of competition. College football has its Heisman Trophy. Golf honors include the Ryder Cup Team. Professional football has its Pro Bowl. Other sports honor their stars at midseason, as in the All-Star Game in baseball and basketball. There are also Most Valuable Player awards, batting champ awards, the Cy Young Award and others. The point is that we recognize those whose performances are above average.

THE MVP CATEGORY OF MANHOOD

What classification do we have for men who have learned to excel in their God-given community responsibilities of being providers, pastors and protectors?

Once a man has achieved a measure of consistent success at loving his wife, raising his children responsibly, demonstrating credibility in his professional and personal affairs—once he has a measured track record—what now for him? Are there any other heights to climb on the ladder of community responsibility?

Yes, there is one. Scripture denotes a final rung on the ladder of responsibility that all men are invited to achieve—the position of *patriarch*.

What do I mean? What is a patriarch? It is, I admit, an archaic, mostly forgotten word today. What does it mean and does it really have any relevance for us in the twenty-first century?

The English definition of *patriarch*, as defined by *Webster's Dictionary*, is "the father and ruler of a family or tribe, as one of the founders.... A person regarded as the founder or father of a colony, religion, business, etc.... A man of great age and dignity." A patriarch is recognized as the leader of a particular community, especially as it applies to family viability.

Many of the great figures of the Old Testament, such as Abraham, Isaac, Jacob, Joseph and David, are known as patriarchs. Many other "chief princes" (Hebrew: *nasi*) provided tribal leadership and helped to govern the nation through their particular community.[3] Though Abraham and Jacob receive most of the attention in the New Testament for their performance as exemplary leaders of their people as patriarchs, the concept of a patriarch was an ideal to which every man was to aspire as he aged and took on more responsibility within his family for their social, economic, spiritual and security needs.

This was the role of a biblical patriarch. This role included not only the leadership of a family but also the maturity to provide modeling and influence to younger men, to offer wisdom for making prudent decisions and to provide sufficient resources for those under their care. Though there would naturally be different elevations of influence, the principles remained the same for each man who led his clan. So the patriarch essentially was a day-to-day hero, living out his God-given role before his family, clan and greater community as a conscientious tribal leader.

That kind of leadership is important because God's wisdom for individuals is to call them into community. He knows that it is not good for us to be alone (Genesis 2:18) and that isolation breeds disaster. So he conceived a plan for our general health and welfare—the idea of family relationships within the context of a greater community, especially a spiritual community. For the Israelites it was their nation of "chosen people." And for us it is the church, the body of Christ.

Dave Dewitt, author of *The Mature Man*, helps us appreciate the significance of patriarchs' stature with the following comments.

> These are "men who wanted to be, not only fathers but shepherds of extended families." . . . A patriarch is a man who has taken on the responsibility for establishing maturity for himself and applying it to his extended family. . . . The patriarch is the highest calling of a man on earth. He is the basis of all societies, religions and nations. Without the patriarch, all social structures fail.[4]

This can be seen biblically in Genesis 26—46 with the life of Jacob. He grew into this role of patriarch, but he sure didn't start there! In fact, his beginnings were rather dishonorable and inauspicious. His disreputable start began when he deceived and negotiated his brother out of his inheritance. Then in complicity with his mother, he lied to his aging father in order to seal the deception and guarantee the inheritance. It worked but it almost cost him his life. Ultimately he was forced into exile, departing from his homeland and fearing for his life, his brother Esau having vowed to kill him for his offenses (Genesis 27:41).

But in a foreign and hostile land God tempered Jacob's character, forming him into a man of maturity and responsibility ready to take the helm as his family's tribal head. Therefore, when he finally remigrated to the land of promise, taking up residence and tribal leadership there, he was able to successfully establish his family roots in this new homeland. Later, as prophesied, the progeny of his twelve sons, the twelve tribes, would one day occupy the land of Palestine, casting aside the pagan inhabitants' nations and turning it into Israel, a nation set apart for God's purposes.

That brings us back to our story with Boaz and Ruth, who were living in this very region. One, Boaz, an Israelite in the tradition of Jacob—a budding tribal leader, a patriarch. The other, Ruth, another vulnerable female like Tamar, looking to the grace of God for deliverance from her pagan past through the mercy and strength of God's noble men (Joshua 6:25).

A patriarch's stature isn't merely the result of a blood relationship to a particular tribe. Nor is it gained simply by the longevity of his life. It's based upon performance. A patriarch is a man who has earned the veneration of his clan because of his wisdom, leadership, involvement and concern for the health and welfare of his people. He maintains the continuity of his people and secures the best possible lifestyle for them now, while seeking the next generation's prosperity in the future. He is a man that everyone in the community can look up to for leadership and inspiration.

That is just the kind of guy Boaz was. It is just the kind of man the communities of America desperately need. And it is just the kind of character our families deserve from us. Let's look again at Boaz's example.

Ruth 4

[1] Now Boaz went up to the gate and sat down there, and behold, the close relative of whom Boaz spoke was passing by, so he said, "Turn aside, friend, sit down here." And he turned aside and sat down.
[2] He took ten men of the elders of the city and said, "Sit down here." So they sat down.

³ Then he said to the closest relative, "Naomi, who has come back from the land of Moab, has to sell the piece of land which belonged to our brother Elimelech.
⁴ "So I thought to inform you, saying, 'Buy it before those who are sitting here, and before the elders of my people. If you will redeem it, redeem it; but if not, tell me that I may know; for there is no one but you to redeem it, and I am after you.'" And he said, "I will redeem it."
⁵ Then Boaz said, "On the day you buy the field from the hand of Naomi, you must also acquire Ruth the Moabitess, the widow of the deceased, in order to raise up the name of the deceased on his inheritance."
⁶ The closest relative said, "I cannot redeem it for myself, because I would jeopardize my own inheritance. Redeem it for yourself; you may have my right of redemption, for I cannot redeem it."
⁷ Now this was the custom in former times in Israel concerning the redemption and the exchange of land to confirm any matter: a man removed his sandal and gave it to another; and this was the manner of attestation in Israel.
⁸ So the closest relative said to Boaz, "Buy it for yourself." And he removed his sandal.
⁹ Then Boaz said to the elders and all the people, "You are witnesses today that I have bought from the hand of Naomi all that belonged to Elimelech and all that belonged to Chilion and Mahlon.
¹⁰ "Moreover, I have acquired Ruth the Moabitess, the widow of Mahlon, to be my wife in order to raise up the name of the deceased on his inheritance, so that the name of the deceased will not be cut off from his brothers or from the court of his

birth place; you are witnesses today."

11 All the people who were in the court, and the elders, said, "We are witnesses. May the LORD make the woman who is coming into your home like Rachel and Leah, both of whom built the house of Israel; and may you achieve wealth in Ephrathah and become famous in Bethlehem.

12 "Moreover, may your house be like the house of Perez whom Tamar bore to Judah, through the offspring which the LORD will give you by this young woman."

13 So Boaz took Ruth, and she became his wife, and he went in to her. And the LORD enabled her to conceive, and she gave birth to a son.

14 Then the women said to Naomi, "Blessed is the LORD who has not left you without a redeemer today, and may his name become famous in Israel.

15 "May he also be to you a restorer of life and a sustainer of your old age; for your daughter-in-law, who loves you and is better to you than seven sons, has given birth to him."

16 Then Naomi took the child and laid him in her lap, and became his nurse.

17 The neighbor women gave him a name, saying, "A son has been born to Naomi!" So they named him Obed. He is the father of Jesse, the father of David.

Boaz, a Community MVP

The Hebrew legal environment, within which this ancient story is set, was very different than the courts that we are familiar with in our culture. Their courtroom was the city gate.[5] Their constitution was the Mosaic law, especially the Pentateuch (the first five books of the Bible). Their court officials were elders, senior members of the community. Their contracts were verbal, and the document of attestation was a sandal! This signified the new owner's right to "walk on the property."

Most interesting to me are the fine points of this transaction. The acquisition of property was economically quantifiable. But in the fine print of this deal are the details of virtue and volition that were needed to accept the "liability" that went with the acquisition. See, the situation here was a twofold commitment and therefore a double problem.

The first issue was the need of the widow Naomi to sell the family property. She could not provide a living for herself as she was unable to till the land. So up for sale it went. But as I've mentioned before the Jewish constitution required that the property stay in the family (Leviticus 25:25). And the "law of the levirate"[6] required that the family member who acquired the property would become liable to father a son for the deceased widow, so that the deceased name would continue within the clan. That was the second problem for this transaction.

These two laws, archaic and perhaps senseless to us, were God's means to maintain clan continuity. They provided that a family's property, though sold, would not be consumed by a non-family member's real estate holdings, thereby erasing the previous family's potential wealth, future inheritance and economic/social position in the community.[7] And the levirate law provided for clan continuity by ensuring that a man's name and therefore legacy would continue into succeeding generations through a physical heir. Otherwise the family name would be lost by the untimely death of a married man who had not yet fathered a son.

These two requirements suddenly took the glitter off the deal for the unnamed "kinsman" in Ruth 4. Instead of the immediate growth of his personal estate by the acquisition of a dead man's property, he now saw that the deal was connected to the deceased living widow and her daughter-in-law. This meant that he would not only have to care for her, requiring that this new property be economically productive, but he was not really going to enjoy ownership of the land, only a fiduciary responsibility to till it and keep it until the male he sired through the widow's daughter-in-law was of age to take the property as his own. Plus the sired male would also become blood-related to this kinsman and would have a share of the family's inheritance as a half-brother to any other males in the kinsman's household!

The only way this kinsman could benefit financially from this arrangement was if the widow was childless (no daughters-in-law either) and unable to bear children. Then upon her death the property would revert to the kinsman, as the nearest relative to the widow. That wasn't the case here. Though Naomi was beyond childbearing years, her daughter-in-law wasn't. The kinsman saw the financial noose he was about to stick his head into and backed out. In sum, to the kinsman this deal was a net loss. It was a commitment to care for a widow and any children Ruth bore without any remuneration for these services. Not a very good business deal but a necessary humanitarian deal if he cared about the health and welfare of Elimelech's kin. Apparently he didn't, for he forfeited the acquisition to Boaz, offering his sandal to him as proof that he wanted no part in the deal (Ruth 4:8).

Boaz gladly, quickly and thoroughly accepted the transaction. Then he consummated the purchase and married Ruth in order to "raise up the name of the deceased" (4:5), heir to both his and Elimelech's family properties. As a result, redemptive history gained a crucial link to the Messiah.

Trying to Relate

Is this a little much for your contemporary tastes? Is a three-thousand-year-old tradition too hard to relate to, especially when we are trying to glean some principles for being patriarchs today? I understand. I have the same difficulty trying to relate to ancient cultures even when there are fewer years involved and they involve my country.

Take George Washington for instance. Can you relate to him personally? I find it hard to. But think about him. It has been so many generations since he lived that he is hardly a memory. It is hard to imagine someone in any kind of relatable terms who lived over two hundred years ago. How did he speak? How did he walk? How did he dress, and what is with the wig thing and all the ruffles, anyway?

But history tells us he was a great man. He was leader of the Continental Army during the American Revolution and mastermind of the military strategies that helped us win our freedom as an independent nation from England. He was tough, tempered, religious, fair and strategically brilliant. But it is still hard to catch a living vision of this guy as a man, one of us. You know what I mean? To me he is just the guy on the U.S. dollar bill and the one who could "not tell a lie. It was I, father, who cut down the cherry tree."

I guess that is why I took notice when I read Abigail Adams's account of her impressions of our first president. He became more relevant, relatable and genuinely impressive.

Abigail, whose husband, John, was languishing in the role of the first vice president, could have taken a competitor's perspective, jealous for the reputation of her husband. But she didn't. She spoke so highly of Washington that I figure he must really have been something special. He seemed to actually be fulfilling the role of a patriarch for our newborn country.

Listen to Abigail Adams as she speaks of our first president when confronted with an awkward social situation involving her, the vice president's wife.

> The President never failed to see the situation corrected without anyone being offended. He has so happy a faculty of appearing to accommodate and yet carrying his point that if he was not really one of the best-intentioned men in the world, he might be a very dangerous one.
>
> He is polite with dignity, affable without formality, distant without haughtiness, grave without austerity, modest, wise and good. These are traits in his character which peculiarly fit him for the exalted station he holds, and God grant that he may hold it with the same applause and universal satisfaction for many, many years, as it is my firm opinion that no other man could rule over this great people and consolidate them into one mighty empire but he who is set over us.[8]

Wow. She pays him the highest compliment a constituent could. Her observations of his behavior help frame for us the characteristics inherent in a patriarch—polite, dignified, modest, wise and good. And she helps us to see the practical influence of historical figures. Thanks, Abigail.

A Patriarch's Relevance for Today

Let's now try to draw some relevance from the situation in Israel, though it took place thousands of years ago, when the judges ruled and men did as they pleased and most ignored the needs of the hurting, except one rare exception, Boaz. Don't sweat the ancient culture, it's the principles that matter most for you and me. I believe the principles are actually fairly easy to glean, if perhaps harder to implement!

First, Boaz didn't waste any time in trying to assist these widows (4:1). Procrastination, more often than not, is a "no" vote, not a "wait till later," as we want to believe.

Second, Boaz went about the whole transaction with integrity, legality, honesty and openness (4:2-5). His faith act, in this situation, was his willingness to accept the results without trying to manipulate them.

Third, Boaz was willing to let others more qualified help if they were so inclined. This was another act of faith coupled with humility. He didn't have to be the big man, whether he truly was or not. He knew his place in the community and accepted it.

Fourth, Boaz's commitment to God, law, these women's welfare and ultimately his wedding proposal, as well as the fruit of his union with Ruth (a son), were an unashamed public affair. He let the community see, enjoy and celebrate this marvelous act of redemption. In doing so, he no doubt elicited the confidence of the city leaders and the appreciation of the neighborhood women as well as the gratitude of his new wife and mother-in-law. Remember, women are relational beings, and part of their sense of security is feeling accepted and included in the interaction of a supporting community.

Boaz was not ashamed of Ruth the Moabitess, nor her and Naomi's pitiful history. He was willing to pay the price for their restoration to life, health, welfare and community. And he was willing to share it all with those interested folks in the neighborhood.

Those are the hallmarks of a patriarch, and they are inspiring. Now let's briefly go back over this, here in our private men's locker room.

A LITTLE SELF-EVALUATION

Men, are you prompt in following through on your commitments to your family, friends, those in your profession and to your God? Or do you procrastinate, forget and leave a trail of broken promises and forgotten pledges in your wake?

Are you public in your commitments? If you are living with some girl, why don't you marry her? If you are proud of her and the life you will build together, why not marry her in a public setting like a church rather than elope to Las Vegas? Are you afraid of something? Are you man enough to get married? Are you willing to let others in your (and her) clan and community share in that public celebration?

Are you willing to make public commitments at all? Can you envision yourself as a man who stands up and steps forward to endorse a cause you believe in? Are you willing to be associated with a minority, if it's the right cause, in order to engender confidence in others to join the cause as well?

A TEXAS-SIZED INSPIRATION

One spring break, I took my family to the Alamo in San Antonio, Texas. While visiting the restored fortress we watched a movie portraying the men and the final days of their defense of that church, which stood in the way of the advancing battalions of the Mexican army. That film brought that ancient memory as well as that historical monument to life!

I shall never forget Colonel Travis's challenge to the men at the Alamo. He drew a line in the sand and called the men to step forward if they were willing to stay and fight the approaching invaders. These family men, fighting beside their fellow countrymen, knew that they were facing certain death. They knew if they left the compound, they stood a fair chance of escaping and staying alive. But they also knew that the Alamo's defense required as many men as possible. The stand at the Alamo was crucial to the overall success of the new republic of Texas. Travis and his men were buying critical time for Sam Houston to marshal troops for a legitimate Texas army to face Santa Ana's overwhelming forces. These ordinary men in the Alamo knew that the entire republic was at stake.

What drama, as man after man stepped across the line to proclaim publicly their stake in the fight. That step of commitment meant they were willing to pay the ultimate price to buy time to secure a healthy future for their fellow countrymen. They knew that such a public testimony was undeniable and irreversible. What an example. What an inspiration!

That's the power of a public testimony. That's the benefit of taking a public stand on important but debated matters. It engenders confidence in others, and it helps hold us accountable to vows we make but may hedge on when times get tough.

Boaz would have fought well at the Alamo, or at Valley Forge, or in our culture today. He was a man who knew the right thing to do and how to announce it to the community for their inspiration. The results of his stand for virtue, redemption and service unified an entire community and blessed a special family.

YOUR TURN

So how about you? Are you willing to be more outspoken about what you believe in and become more involved in your community?

How do you react to competitors for the welfare of your clan? Are you willing to go to bat for your girl? Does your wife or girlfriend know that you'll go to any extreme to defend her in public? Will you defuse all suitors and confront every competitor to your relationship because she is that valuable to you? Boaz did!

Are you willing to pay the price it takes to secure the heath and welfare of your family and extended family? Even if it means no new golf clubs, less savings, fewer hours in front of the TV and time instead helping a family member get their act together, as inconvenient as it may be?

Being a patriarch is redemptive. It's heroic! It costs to be the one at the top. In fact, by definition, it will cost you what you don't want to pay because an easy cost is no real cost at all. Superficial sacrifices didn't buy much then and they don't buy much now.

The unnamed kinsman in our story ultimately was no kinsman at all. He proved to be just another selfish, self-protective family member. He missed his opportunity to lead, to serve, to give, to save. He forfeited a memorial in history, a chance to make a difference—to be a patriarch. As a result, his name has slipped off the pages of the biblical record, never to be mentioned again.

Ah, but the valiant warrior Boaz, the real man in this story, stepped up and met the challenge. He paid the redemption price[9] for two women, and as a result not only is he the hero of this story, his legacy will live on to eternity. For through his marriage to Ruth and the subsequent birth of their son, a lineage continued until the stream of heredity resulted in the birth and subsequent coronation of the great king, David. Through David the Messianic lineage continued until its genetic stream pooled in fruition in the birth of a greater King, our Savior Jesus Christ, the King of Kings.[10]

Men, this is what being a man of honor is all about. It's about pioneering relational frontiers and piercing social barriers to be good stewards of the areas God has set before us relationally, financially and morally. That is what God intends for males to do with their masculinity. We are to use our gender strengths for the success, security and stability of our families and communities. That's our role!

So let's stand up, take the challenge and serve the needs of our families and neighbors through the resources God has given us. Let's do so with selfless abandon, integrity, love, truth and generosity.

Then, no doubt, we'll see God work in ways that enhance and bless everyone in our circle of influence.

That is what being a man is, a male who acts responsibly. That is what being a patriarch is, a man who lives redemptively with every fiber of his being and every resource within his stewardship. All the effort is for the glory of God. Therefore the cost is worth it.

By now we've received enough instruction to try this and enough practice to succeed. So it's game time. It is time to leave the locker room and impact our world for good, for God.

A Time to Proceed and to Persevere

How do you want to be remembered? Have you thought about it, or do you even care? Obviously, you and I won't be here forever. But what we do here counts twice on our scorecard.

The first is temporal. The people you touch and the lives you leave behind will be better or worse off for how you affected them. Remember Jimmy Stewart's role in *It's a Wonderful Life*. In that Frank Capra film, Stewart as George Bailey was given an unusual opportunity. An angel gave him the chance to see how his friends and neighborhood would have turned out if he had never lived. What he saw was so dark and frightening that it shook him from his suicidal thinking and remotivated him to make a difference in his community. It is similar for you. What you do has a positive or negative effect on those in your path. That effect will live on in their lives long after you are gone.

The second fact is equally sobering. What you do now actually will follow you to heaven, and you will be either rewarded or ashamed for your efforts here (1 Corinthians 3:14-15). In the movie *Gladiator* Russell Crowe plays the general of the Roman armies of the north, Maximus Decimus Meridius. Early in the movie Maximus marshals his army for a final great contest against the last stronghold of opposition to the spread of the Roman Empire. If Rome could defeat these Germanic warriors, the world would be theirs. Peace would at last reign throughout the kingdom. So in an inspiring "pre-game pep talk" to his cavalry, Maximus rallies his men, saying, *"Remember, what you do in this life echoes in eternity."*

Gosh, I really love that line. It's a pump-up reminder of what is really important—eternity. Though we can't see it now, it's coming soon enough whether we are ready or not.

Finishing the Race

It is the 1968 Olympics in Mexico City. The marathon, one of the most prestigous events of the games, is in progress and a buzz of excitement fills the streets as the runners slip gracefully by. Hopefuls such as Mamo Wolde of Ethiopia, Kenji Kimihara of Japan and Michael Ryan from New Zealand[11] run with grace and strategic intent, easing their way through the winding course, past the cheering spectators as they stride toward the finish. That line, some twenty-six miles away, is ensconced in an athletic stadium filled with eighty thousand expectant fans. As the first runners draw near, the electricity from those fans is palpable, escalating in intensity as the entire stadium of onlookers rises to greet the arrival of the first runners across the finish line.

However, toward the end of the pack, a lone Tanzanian runner by the name of John Stephen Akwari is bringing up the rear. He is not expected to compete for a medal, but he is the one entrant from his proud country. Somewhere along the route he falls, cuts himself and has to be bandaged by the medical staff following the event.

Much later, he actually enters the stadium. He is so far behind the other competitors that the arena is nearly empty. There is no great chorus of cheers from the spectators. A few stunned fans applaud politely as he stumbles around the remaining four hundred meters of cinderblock track before falling over the finish line.

Exhausted, bloodied, bruised and bandaged, the bewildered marathoner is jolted to his senses by the intrusive question of an insensitive journalist. Sticking a microphone in Akwari's face, the incredulous reporter asks, "What in the world would behoove a man to put himself through such hell in order to finish this race?"

Without hesitation Akwari retorted, "My country didn't send me five thousand miles to start this race. They sent me five thousand miles to finish it."[12]

Wow, you can't argue with his logic. Nor can you ignore his grit. How about you?

God sent his Son from heaven to earth to give you eternal life and to start you on the road to success as a man, a husband, a father, a neighbor and a citizen. All he asks you to do is stand up, whether you are bruised by life of not, and by faith follow him to the finish line of responsible living. Can we do it? Yes, we can!

Will he give us the strength to turn mere boys into valiant warriors like Boaz for his redemptive purposes? You bet he will.

So will we let him? Will we follow him? Will we choose to live responsibly as providers, pastors, protectors and patriarchs? Will we get up, get going and finish this race, not to beat all contestants but to represent our families well? Will we choose manhood? Will we choose the battlefield or will we wilt under pressure and quit, choosing the couch and the remote over the contest?

Men, it's time to choose whether you will be a wimp or a warrior, merely a male or a real man.

AFTERWORD

This book was born out of painful personal experience that forced me to reckon with what God requires of a man of honor. After a career change that involved a relocation, I discovered that I had seriously upset the stability applecart at home. The tension was so bad that I was tempted to believe that ignoring family needs might be a better solution than addressing the challenges I had created.

Fortunately, my faith, the Lord and the people I love gave me the impetus I needed to continue to work on family stability. Rather than ignore the challenges at home, which would have compounded one bad decision with another, I went on a research and rescue mission in Scripture. In those days of mental and emotional fatigue, I desperately needed clear direction on the issue of male responsibility to redirect my path more successfully.

Past Bible reading had put the pitiful example of Elimelech in the back of my mind. I knew what he had done. I didn't want to replicate his mistakes, so I went back to the book of Ruth to see if there was a biblical alternative to the Elimelech syndrome. There was! It was Boaz.

I chose to follow Boaz's example. I redoubled my commitment to the true things of value—my God and Savior, my wife and kids, my role and responsibilities. Living in anticipation of God's deliverance and guidance has illuminated for me this critical component of successful stewarding. All of this adds up to becoming a man of honor.

I hope the thoughts I've shared from my experience and study of Scripture have been helpful to you. I hope what you've read so far has been as instructive and inspiring to you as I found it to be for me. But we are not done. Before my thesis is complete I must share with you one last critical component for the construction of a man of honor. I hope these final thoughts help you get a clear sense of direction as you recalibrate your compass to make sure you are on the correct path in life.

I said earlier that sometimes God calls a man to unmoor his boat from the familiar in order to set out into the horizon of his directed adventure. I also said that we should be careful, remember? Well, setting our own course in life can get us in over our heads in a hurry. I found that out the hard way too.

A Bad Day of Boating

While in college on the West Coast, I took a job at a marina. It was a facility for repairing and selling both new and used yachts. While there, my roommate moved out so I had to find either another roommate or a smaller apartment. But I had a better idea. I bought one of the yachts the marina had for sale, refinished it and moved on board, making it my new living quarters. I felt that building equity in my "live-aboard yacht" was preferable to flushing rent down the drain every month with an apartment.

In other words I became a boat owner for economic reasons, not because I was a mariner.

I soon found out that boat ownership netted one a lot of new friends, especially lady friends. So I regularly entertained a load of new friends aboard my floating party barge as we tooled around the marina.

Then one Saturday I got an even brighter idea. I would take a young lady whom I was trying to impress to Catalina Island for a day of fun in the sun. The only problem was that I was no navigational expert and had never previously motored the twenty-five-plus miles to the lone island west of Long Beach Marina.

The day began wonderfully. We headed out beyond the breakwater and set our compass northwest on the heading I had been told would put us squarely onto the island's eastern beach at Avalon Bay on the Catalina southern coast. Unfortunately the weather abruptly turned bad, and rain began to pelt my yacht. Not to worry. I turned on my windshield wipers and kept heading out into the great blue sea.

But as I looked down to check our heading, I noticed that my electric compass was going haywire, spinning crazily and uncontrollably in circles! Yikes. Without a compass we couldn't be sure of our direction. This was critical. If we missed Catalina Island there was no landmass beyond to block our path out into deeper water and landless sea. Suddenly my day turned from fun to fright.

I purposely stopped the boat dead in the water. I wasn't going to risk running by that island. But the problem was far from solved. I was simply trying to avert a bigger problem while my mind went into overdrive seeking a solution.

My boat contained two fifty-gallon tanks of fuel but only got about two nautical miles per gallon. So if I motored past our destination, we could be well out to sea before we knew it and find we didn't have enough fuel to return. We wouldn't be sure of our direction anyway. Plus we had very little food or water on board. So another scenario I wanted to avoid was several days at sea with the anchor out, floating like a cork.

I didn't like the prospect of winging it with navigation, and I knew my date wasn't interested in my luck. So I let the boat idle in the water, hoping to catch a sense of the swell direction, which was running southeast that time of year. I figured if we headed directly into the prevailing swell we would be generally heading in a northwesterly direction. I used to surf a lot in those days and prided myself in the ability to discern swell direction, so I thought I could do that out at sea as well. But I was way wrong!

The clouds had descended around our position. We couldn't see a hundred feet in front of us. As I stuck my head out of the canvas overhang that sheltered the bridge, I discovered that I couldn't tell swell direction at all. The wind was blowing one way, the swells were coming from a different direction, and the rain seemed to be coming from every direction! We were directionless, and it was my responsibility to get us out of this fix. And the sooner the better, before we drifted into further trouble.

In those days I wasn't much in the habit of prayer. But I recall a quick shot heavenward that day asking my creator for some help. And soon, if that would be okay! Honestly, I didn't know what else to do.

Soon the rain stopped and the skies began to clear. Whew. But still no compass. Now what?

Maybe, I thought, *if the clouds will clear enough for me to see the coast line behind us, we can call this a day and at least head back to shore and the safety of the marina . . .* or so my survival instincts groped for hope.

In preparation to do that, as the clouds lifted, I re-fired the engines, turned the windshield wipers off—and my compass was working again! We were saved! We had reliable direction again.

It seems that the windshield wipers had shorted the circuitry to the electric compass, causing it to spin wildly. Once the power to the wipers was off, the compass regained its calibration and we could confidently use it to find our heading. With a working compass, we were off to Avalon Bay and had what ended up being a wonderful day. But without that compass, not only would our Catalina holiday have been impossible, simply regaining safety would have been a challenge too.

Off Course in Life?

Life is like that. You can motor off confidently seeking a good old-fashioned time and suddenly a life storm seizes your attention. Then the ensuing chaos short circuits your sense of direction. The next thing you know, a fairly normal obstacle turns into an insurmountable hurdle, threatening to throw your normal way of life far off course, causing you more pain than you ever imagined the initial risk could involve.

When that happens, the Enemy will show up offering a subtle option to your mess, a temptation to take a shortcut. If that shortcut involves sin—my friend, take it from me—your trip into trouble has just begun!

One author I appreciate has warned of these troubling episodes this way: "Sin will take you farther than you want to go, sin will keep you longer than you want to stay, sin will cost you more than you want to pay."[1]

I am so glad that on that fateful day of adventure yachting, I decided to stay put and pray until a solution arrived rather than rely on my own native instincts. My so-called ability to discern swell direction would have doomed us to a two-hundred-mile trip to nowhere. There's no telling how long we would have remained there until we were rescued by the Coast Guard or someone else smarter in nautical navigation than me.

From Boating to Bait

Can you relate? Does any of this sound like you or one of your friends, or perhaps your father or brother?

I believe we get off course in life when we choose a selfish direction for ourselves (which is an act of sin) instead of waiting for the clear direction of God. The challenge is that the temptation is so

Afterword

very subtle at times. We are led astray by impulses that we don't see as harmful or sinful at first. This miscalculation on our part is more complex than the obvious presentation of a sinful substitute to obedience. Getting off course in disobedience is often the abuse or misuse of God-given drives and gifts because of the temporary experience of failure or a certain difficulty in those gift areas. That is what makes temptation so powerful.

We were designed by our creator to experience and to achieve certain things. Intuitively we know that. So when our lives don't measure up (and they never will, since the whole of creation has been subjected to futility—Romans 8:18-23; Ecclesiastes 1:2, 14), our natural yearning for completion and fulfillment gets hungry and assertive. In lieu of success, that appetite wants to be quenched. So we often choose a cheap, quick alternative to satisfy our cravings. That can lead to a very bad decision that results in horrible life circumstances.

This causes many men to underperform their calling. We find ourselves opting for the low road of contemporary living rather than the heroic role of a biblical man. We all have a natural inclination to succeed in the stewardship areas God has gifted us. But when our sense of direction is distorted by failure or fatigue, rediscovering success can become an obsession, becoming a "lust" for the man who perceives himself as a loser in a critical area of fulfillment. That typically is when Satan delivers the bait, the counterfeit "food" that stirs lust into a froth of uncontrollable desire. That can be enough to motivate a man to lunge at the wrong solution, creating sin and causing regret.

When we fall prey to our lusts, we forfeit the real fulfillment of having a unique connection to God *through the trial* and discovering what the apostle Paul called the special fellowship of Christ's sufferings (Philippians 3:7-14). The whole thing is very subtle and very dangerous. As James 1:12-16 says,

> Blessed is a man who perseveres under trial [or temptation]; for once he has been approved, he will receive the crown of life which the Lord has promised to those who love Him. Let no one say when he is tempted, "I am being tempted by God"; for God cannot be tempted by evil, and He Himself does not tempt anyone. But each one is tempted when he is carried away and enticed by *his own lust*. Then when lust has conceived, it gives birth to sin; and when sin is accomplished, it brings forth death. Do not be deceived, my beloved brethren. (italics mine)

I think that is what happened to Elimelech. He wasn't successful in Israel, and he saw a chance for a quick remedy in Moab. Though migration to a foreign country in mistrust of God's provision was prohibited to Jews, he did it anyway and suffered a series of disastrous setbacks for himself, his sons and ultimately the women he was to serve with noble masculinity.

FROM BAIT TO GRACE

Yet God was ever faithful, taking the believing remnant of Elimelech's wife, Naomi, and daughter-in-law, Ruth, back to the security of their homeland, people and the masculine model, Boaz.

I believe God is still that gracious to men such as you and me. We fail from time to time. We are not perfect, not one of us. Some of us have wrecked our lives more than others. Some of us have perhaps done so irrevocably. But remember that God is not one of us. He gives us chance after chance after chance, if we are truly

Afterword

repentant and willing to start over again.

This is also why he warns us against judging others who have failed. He knows our plight. He knows we are susceptible to the deceptions of a powerful enemy. And we fall prey to the world's system, which wars against our spiritual success. But despite our propensity to sin, God freely offers his grace to us in redemption through Christ Jesus (Ephesians 1:7-9). Plus he invites us to experience his forgiveness and to fellowship with him. He demonstrates his mercy despite our imperfections. He gives us what we need, not what we deserve. I like that. I need that!

One of my favorite verses in the New Testament is from the apostle Paul in Philippians 3:13-14: "Forgetting what lies behind and reaching forward to what lies ahead, I press on toward the goal for the prize of the upward call of God in Christ Jesus." When I have spoke on this in chapel to professional sports teams, especially after a horrible loss and before a new contest, I've paraphrased the ideas of this verse as "God asks us to admit it, forget it and move on."

Of course he still wants us to succeed morally. He wants us to succeed obediently, to do the right things the right way. He just doesn't reject us once we've stumbled in trying to execute our stewardship.

He encourages us to persevere with the grace he gives us (Romans 12:12). He provides grace above circumstances and above temporary stewardship failure. Christ invites us to accept his grace of relationship, offering fellowship with the creator of the universe and redeemer of our souls. It is a grace that bids us to delight in the eternal and to find our satisfaction in the spiritual. And it is a grace that cannot be apprehended except by suffering through trial in surrender to God's authority. It is, as Paul recounts, the fellowship of Christ. That is the daily choice we all have, either to know sin or to know him (Philippians 3:7-14).

It's all based on motivation. We have to ask and answer the question, "What really gives me fulfillment?" Do I want a clean conscience, a positive impact on my community and fellowship with God through the risk and pursuit of noble masculinity? Or do I want achievement at any cost to my soul and to others? Before you answer, I pray you will consider another probing question: Does your sense of responsibility before your creator demand that you fulfill your masculine calling? Or are you convinced that contemporary culture sets the compass direction for your life and gender identity? Whose responsibility is it to live right and lead others the right way, yours or someone else's?

A Classic Example of High Achievement

I've mentioned him before, but the more I read about Winston Churchill, the more he reminds me of a patriarch. Churchill was a devoted family man and community leader, and he grew to care, as a true patriarch should, for the welfare of his entire nation. [2]

I admire his drive and balance of family and career. He was not merely content to be a successful politician; he also wanted to be a successful family man. Later he would combine these two honorable intentions as he evolved into a man who sacrificed, led and saved an entire nation of families from the devastating threat of Nazi Germany.

Though he was often maligned, misunderstood and rejected by political opposition in his country, he nevertheless pressed on toward the target of his honorable intent, governing himself, his loved ones and his country for the safety, security and prosperity of all. He was a man of honor by anyone's standards, for sure!

HOW ABOUT YOU, MY FRIEND?

As you consider your calling as a man and the inevitable costs of excellence as you seek to become a man of honor, I encourage you to steel yourself for battle. Being a man of honor has more to do with practicing the right principles than pedigree, as Churchill's example illustrates. Though making a commitment toward being a man of honor isn't easy, what comes next is even harder as it involves a fight. The high and noble decision to use your masculine strength and resources to positively influence your clan, community and country won't come to fruition except through a certain inevitable war.

Where will you fight this battle? Some days that battle is against your own moral sloth. Other days will be skirmishes against other less noble characters who have a vested interest in seeing you fall instead of stand. Satan himself will attack you since he doesn't want you to provide a public model of masculinity contrary to the wimpy models he has prominently displayed in our sin-stained world. There will be other invaders to the territory of honorable intentions. But know this. There is one resource, one person you can always count on. It is your Savior and Lord, Jesus.

If God is a warrior (Exodus 15:3), you can count on him to go to battle with you. Plus the resources that he makes available to you and me in Christ will enable us to be victors and more than conquerors (1 Corinthians 15:57, Romans 8:37) against enemies to our God-given stewardship. So when occasional and inevitable defeats frustrate your godly ambition, our sacred helper, the Lord Jesus, will bid you again to come to him for forgiveness, cleansing, renewal and refocus (1 John 1:9; 3:3; Matthew 11:28-30). I'm so glad he is so available to help and to heal!

God bless you, men, as you proceed in the way of honor as God's representatives to our families and communities.

A Prayer for Men of Honor

Blessed Lord Jesus, thank you for your indescribable gift of grace and for the unalienable gifts of our stewardship. Thanks for this great opportunity for success, for the high calling of biblical masculinity. Help me to be a hero to my wife and family. I pray for grace to represent you to them as a provider, pastor, protector and patriarch. Help me serve my family and community and become the man of honor you want me to be.

In the heroic name of Jesus, Amen.

NOTES

Introduction
[1] "Slain Hero Left Gift For Five Strangers," *Good Morning America*, May 21, 2002, <http://more.abcnews.go.com/sections/gma/goodmorningamerica/gma020521kime_family_donation.html>.

Chapter 1: Healthy Men, Family Heroes
[1] Roy Jenkins, *Churchill: A Biography* (New York: Farrar, Straus & Giroux, 2001), p. 8.
[2] Ibid., p. 11.
[3] Ibid.
[4] Ibid., p. 10.
[5] James Humes, *Churchill, Speaker of the Century*, quoted in Kent Hughes, *Disciplines of a Godly Man* (Wheaton, Ill.: Crossway, 1995), pp. 43-44.
[6] David McCullough, *John Adams* (New York: Simon & Schuster, 2001), pp. 257-58.
[7] Ibid., p. 55.
[8] Ibid., p. 289.
[9] Edmund Morris, *Theodore Rex* (New York: Random House, 2001), pp. 124-25.
[10] Received as a personal note from my dear friend Bill Hendricks, Howard's youngest son, and shared with permission.

Chapter 2: Real Men, Bull Riders or Not
[1] Tom Eisenman declares, "Men today are taught to compete, that winning is to be sought at the expense of all else, human or divine. Men are taught to be independent. To need others is a sign of weakness. Men are taught to be concerned with the goal and tasks at hand, that making progress on or accomplishing some project is more important than developing a relationship." Tom Eisenman, *Temptations Men Face* (Downers Grove, Ill.: InterVarsity Press, 1991), p. 37.
[2] Robert Hicks, quoting Dr. Joy Donald, informs us that "the deformed male as the norm in our society . . . has taken two forms. One is the macho man who deals with his deformity by compensating for his insecurity through acting manly rather than being manly. The other is the feminized deformed male who has given up on being a man and runs away from his manhood; he feels more comfortable on the feminine side of life." Robert Hicks, *Uneasy Manhood* (Nashville: Oliver Nelson, 1991), p. 159.
[3] See Elaine Storkey's magnificent overview of the issue of gender construction and the postmodern feminist movement, as published in her work *Origins of Difference* (Grand Rapids, Mich.: Baker Academic, 2001). I also recommend John Piper and Wayne Grudem's work, *Recovering Biblical Manhood and Womanhood* (Wheaton, Ill.: Crossway, 1991), chapter 16, "Biology: Biological Basis for Gender-Specific Behavior," pp. 280-93, and chapter 18, "Sociology: The Inevitability of Failure: The Assumptions and Implementations of Modern Feminism," pp. 312-31.

[4]Piper and Grudem, *Recovering Biblical Manhood and Womanhood*, pp. 282, 293.
[5]James Dobson, *Bringing Up Boys* (Wheaton, Ill.: Tyndale House, 2001), p. 27.
[6]Again I refer you to the writings of Elaine Storkey's *Origins of Difference* and Piper and Grudem's *Recovering Biblical Manhood and Womanhood*.
[7]Robert Hicks, *Uneasy Manhood*, pp. 156, 157, 166.
[8]*Webster's New World Dictionary* (Cleveland: Collins, 1979).

Chapter 3: A Real Man Is a Provider
[1]While Israel did have some modicum of a welfare safety net (Deut 14:28-29; 24:17-20), security for a widow was primarily the responsibility of the family, not the government. Further, I am convinced that in those decadent times when people did as they pleased (Judg 21:25), the legal provisions from the Mosaic law concerning care for widows and orphans were mostly ignored, along with the rest of God's mandates for his nation. What makes Boaz so remarkable is that he didn't have to do all that he did; he could have ignored Ruth and deferred as the first kinsman redeemer did or taken advantage of her. But he didn't.
[2]P/e ratios or price to earnings ratios are defined as "the ratio of the current market price of a share of stock to the corporation's annual earnings per share" (*Webster's New World Dictionary* [Cleveland: Collins, 1979]).
[3]Susan Miller, *After the Boxes Are Unpacked* (Wheaton, Ill.: Tyndale House, 1995), pp. 15. 114-15, quoting Audrey T. McCollum, *The Trauma of Marriage: Psychological Issues for Women* (Newbury Park, Calif.: Sage, 1990), p. 71. Emphasis added. For anyone considering a move, I recommend reading Miller's book and including its insights in your decision-making process. It's a valuable resource for helping you consider all the facts before making a final decision. If nothing else it will help you make your move with your eyes wide open.
[4]See Garry Friesen and J. Robin Maxsom's *Decision Making and the Will of God* (Portland, Ore.: Multnomah Publishing, 1980).
[5]See Bill Hendricks and the folks at The Giftedness Center for further information on how you too can better grasp your arena for life service through your unique gifts, life experiences, motivational drives, network of relationships and other God-given resources for your success <www.thegiftednesscenter.com>.
[6]Ancient women were in a subservient role to their husbands and dependent on the husband for economic survival. Upon the death of their husband, economic viability required a woman to enter the home of her eldest son and remain there for her care and upkeep (Merrill F. Unger, *Unger's Bible Dictionary* [Chicago: Moody Press, 1979], p. 1166). If a woman had no sons to remarry or with which to live, she entered the home of a near kinsman—brother, uncle or even brother-in-law (who could also execute the duty of a levirate marriage with the widow for the express purpose of raising up a seed to carry on her husband's name and the family inheritance—see Gen 38:11; Deut 25:5-10) (Merrill C. Tenney, gen. ed., *The Zondervan Pictorial Encyclopedia of the Bible* [Grand Rapids, Mich.: Zondervan, 1975], 5:928).

Chapter 4: A Real Man Is a Pastor
[1]Don E. Eberly, *Restoring the Good Society* (Grand Rapids, Mich.: Baker, 1994), pp. 115-17.
[2]From a compilation of articles at <www.pgatour.com> and <www.cnnsi.com> websites.

Notes

[3] John Walvoord and Roy Zuck, *The Bible Knowledge Commentary* (Wheaton, Ill.: Victor, 1985), p. 422.
[4] William Harley, *His Needs, Her Needs* (Grand Rapids, Mich.: Revell, 2001), p. 105.
[5] Stu Weber, *Tender Warrior* (Sisters, Ore.: Multnomah Publishing, 1993), p. 71.

Chapter 5: A Real Man Is a Protector

[1] John Gray, *Men Are from Mars, Women Are from Venus* (New York: Harper Collins, 1992), p. 10.
[2] William Harley, *His Needs, Her Needs* (Grand Rapids, Mich.: Revell, 2001), p. 19.
[3] *Webster's New World Dictionary* differentiates between security and stability as follows: Security is "1. The state of being or feeling secure; freedom from fear, anxiety, danger, doubt, etc. 2. Something that gives or assures safety, tranquility, certainty, etc. 3. Protection or defense against attack, interference." Stability is "1. The state or quality of being stable or fixed; steadfast. 2. Firmness of character, purpose, or resolutions."
[4] James Dobson, *Bringing Up Boys* (Wheaton, Ill.: Tyndale House, 2001), p. 27.
[5] Some recent popular men's literature, like *Men's Journal* for example, may make a different claim, suggesting that women are just as sexually aggressive as men, but my observation and *Men's Journal's* own polling comments relay the fact that their samples are from a very small number and probably taken from people predisposed to a minority viewpoint on the issue to begin with. In other words, some of the recent magazine articles that propose a new guideline for understanding sexual expectation are in fact presenting more propaganda than fact. Modern literature often doesn't represent the broader society or the average woman's opinion when she is asked to prioritize her needs in a relationship. See "The New Rules on Sex" by Ariel Cevy in *Men's Journal*, September 2002, pp. 61-71, 136.
[6] See Merrill Unger's comments on this subject in *Unger's Bible Dictionary* (Chicago: Moody Press, 1979), p. 700.
[7] See comments by Walvoord and Zuck, *Bible Knowledge Commentary*, pp. 424-25.
[8] Note this quotation from a respected friend of mine, Tim Parker, pastor of ministry development at Grace Community Church in Roswell, New Mexico, whom I owe some insight into the Christian community's singles scene. Tim comments, "As someone who has worked in leadership of large twentysomething singles groups, I have found several common denominators. First, you are bringing together a melting pot of hundreds of people, both male and female, whose backgrounds and pasts contain various moral and sexual limits and boundaries.

"Second, although we commonly think of the male 'shark' as one who peruses singles groups looking for his next relationship 'fix' or cheap dating service, there are quite an equal number of female 'sharks' looking for the same thing.

"Third, just as Eve rationalized with the serpent as to what God said about eating fruit from the tree, so we rationalize about what the Word of God says in regards to sexual purity and biblical boundaries within relationships with the opposite sex.

"A shocking thought is that I had one pastor tell me that when HIV education was taking off and when a 'certain President of the United States' claimed that oral sex wasn't really sex, a not so surprising thing happened. People wanted to maintain their purity, especially the females, so for not just safety reasons, vaginal intercourse was becoming less 'casual.' What he saw taking off was the incidence of oral sex related illness and disease transmission.

"What it really comes down to is this, sex is sex and arousal is arousal . . . *when* sexual thoughts and feelings are being rationalized to meet our 'need' we cheapen what the Lord outlined for our *dating* relationships" (italics mine).
[9]Remember A. C. Green of the Los Angeles Lakers, for example?
[10]See my comments in *Man of Influence* (Downers Grove, Ill.: InterVarsity Press, 2001), pp. 147-51.

Chapter 6: A Real Man Is a Patriarch
[1]"Stunned Racing World Reacts to Loss," ESPN.com news services, February 23, 2001. Accessed at <http://espn.go.com/classic/s/2001/0222/1101924.html>.
[2]Deb Williams, "For Dale," in *Winston Cup Scene* 24, no. 42, March 1, 2001, pp. 14, 51.
[3]See such examples in Scripture as Exodus 16:22, Numbers 1:16, Joshua 22:30, Judges 5:2 and 1 Kings 8:1.
[4]Dave Dewitt, *The Mature Man* (Portland, Ore.: Multnomah Publishing, 2000), pp. 11, 13, 181.
[5]John Reed, *Bible Knowledge Commentary*, p. 426.
[6]See J. S. Wright and J. A. Thompson, "Marriage," in *New Bible Dictionary*, ed. I. Howard Marshall, A. R. Millard, J. I. Packer and D. J. Wiseman, 3rd ed. (Downers Grove, Ill.: InterVarsity Press, 1996), p. 735.
[7]Edward F. Campbell Jr., in his commentary on Ruth in the Anchor Bible Commentary series (New York: Doubleday, 1975), p. 136.
[8]David McCullough, *John Adams* (New York: Simon & Schuster, 2001), p. 413.
[9]See the definition of redemption in Leon Morris, "Redeemer, Redemption," *New Bible Dictionary*, p. 1003.
[10]See Matthew 1:1-16.
[11]These three men were the eventual gold, silver and bronze medalists for the marathon at the 1968 Olympics.
[12]John Steinbreder, "Olympic Watch," *Sky Magazine*, September 2001, p. 86.

Afterword
[1]Ron Mehl, *Surprise Endings* (Sisters, Ore.: Multnomah Publishing, 1993), p. 91.
[2]Roy Jenkins, *Churchill* (New York: Farrar, Straus & Giroux, 2001), pp. 8-11.

If you enjoyed this book and would like to multiply its impact, Masters Men can help you through a proven method for helping men start successful small groups. We would love to have you join our growing team. For information contact us at P.O. Box 797353, Dallas, TX 75379, or at our website: <www.mastersmenteam.com>.